D0131137

LIVING IN BALI

PHOTOS RETO GUNTLI / TEXT ANITA LOCOCO

Living in Bali

EDITED BY / HERAUSGEGEBEN VON / SOUS LA DIRECTION DE

ANGELIKA TASCHEN

TASCHEN

HONG KONG KÖLN LONDON LOS ANGELES MADRID PARIS TOKYO

Bali Sea

Pemuteran

Ketapang

Gilimanuk

Bali Barat
National Park

Indian Ocean

0   5   10   15   20
KM

JAVA

N

BALI

MT. Batur (1,717m)

Lake Batur

MT. Agung (3,142m)

Lombok Strait

Begawan

Sidemen

Ubud

Sayan

Nyuh Kuning

Padangbai

Lombok

LOMBOK

Kaba-Kaba

Badung Strait

Denpasar
(Capital)

Pabean

Ped

Nusa Lembongan

Batujimbar

Pantai Seseh

Nusa Ceningan

Canggu   Semer
Sanur

Umalas

NUSA PENIDA

Seminyak

Ngurah Rai
International Airport

Benoa

Bukit Peninsula

Pecatu

Uluwatu Temple

Contents / Inhalt / Sommaire

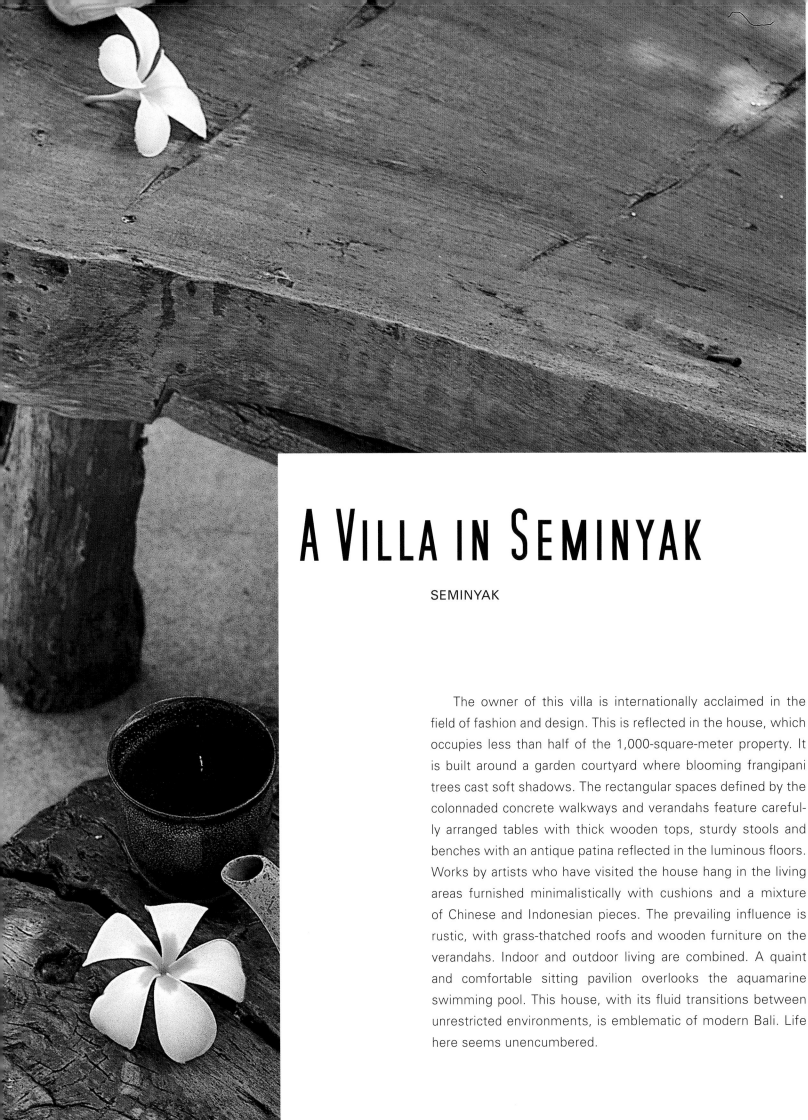

A Villa in Seminyak

SEMINYAK

The owner of this villa is internationally acclaimed in the field of fashion and design. This is reflected in the house, which occupies less than half of the 1,000-square-meter property. It is built around a garden courtyard where blooming frangipani trees cast soft shadows. The rectangular spaces defined by the colonnaded concrete walkways and verandahs feature carefully arranged tables with thick wooden tops, sturdy stools and benches with an antique patina reflected in the luminous floors. Works by artists who have visited the house hang in the living areas furnished minimalistically with cushions and a mixture of Chinese and Indonesian pieces. The prevailing influence is rustic, with grass-thatched roofs and wooden furniture on the verandahs. Indoor and outdoor living are combined. A quaint and comfortable sitting pavilion overlooks the aquamarine swimming pool. This house, with its fluid transitions between unrestricted environments, is emblematic of modern Bali. Life here seems unencumbered.

The natural textures of the outdoor tables, benches and stools of tamarind wood are of simple and understated designs following the grains and patterns of this native African wood.

Die im Freien stehenden Tische, Bänke und Hocker aus Tamarindenholz sind schlicht und unauffällig im Design, wodurch die natürliche Maserung und Musterung dieses ursprünglich afrikanischen Holzes hervorgehoben wird.

Le design minimaliste des tables, bancs et tabourets de jardin taillés dans du bois de tamarin respecte le grain et les veinures de cette essence d'origine africaine.

Diese Villa steht auf einem 1.000 Quadratmeter großen Grundstück und hat ein grünes Herz: Sie wurde rund um einen zauberhaften Patio gebaut, in dem duftende Jasminbäume wachsen, die und für ein faszinierendes Spiel aus Licht und Schatten sorgen. Unter den Kolonnaden und in den Räumen gruppieren sich Tische, Stühle und Bänke aus massivem Holz. Dass die Besitzerin einen internationalen Ruf in der Mode- und Designbranche genießt, erkennt man an den zahlreichen Werken befreundeter Künstler und an den Möbeln aus China sowie Indonesien, die den Wohnbereichen puristisches Flair verleihen. Traumhafte Terrassen lassen Innen- und Außenräume wie selbstverständlich miteinander verschmelzen – ein Lieblingsplatz ist der grasgedeckte Pavillon, von dem man auf den aquamarinblau leuchtenden Swimming-Pool blickt. In dieser Villa zeigt Bali sein modernes Gesicht und fasziniert mit einer ganz besonderen Leichtigkeit des Seins.

Styliste et designer de renommée internationale, la propriétaire a créé une maison caractéristique de la Bali moderne, avec des transitions fluides entre différents environnements dans lesquels on évolue sans entraves. Située sur une propriété de 1 000 mètres carrés, la villa occupe moins de la moitié de cette superficie. Elle est construite autour d'une cour-jardin agrémentée de frangipaniers. Les espaces rectangulaires et les vérandas à colonnades sont sobrement meublés de tables à plateau épais, de tabourets et de bancs dont la patine ancienne reflète les sols d'un blanc lumineux. Des œuvres d'art réalisées par des amis artistes lors de séjours à la propriété sont accrochées dans les espaces de vie agrémentés de coussins et de mobiliers chinois et indonésiens minimalistes. Le toit recouvert de chaume d'alang alang et les meubles en bois des vérandas apportent une note rustique, établissant un lien entre l'intérieur et l'extérieur. Un pavillon original douillettement aménagé invite au repos au bord de la piscine.

LEFT ABOVE:
The bale, a Balinese style sitting pavilion, offsets the terrazzo used for the pool, in which chips of mirror are embedded.

LEFT BELOW:
An old wooden wheel from a horse-drawn cart serves as a decorative symbol on the back wall of the bale.

RIGHT:
Frangipani trees shade a poolside lounge chair hewn from a single slab of wood.

LINKS OBEN:
Ein bale *genannter Sitzpavillon balinesischen Stils steht am mit Terrazzo ausgekleideten Pool.*

LINKS UNTEN:
Das alte Holzrad eines Pferdewagens gibt ein dekoratives Element an der Rückwand des bale-*Pavillons ab.*

RECHTE SEITE:
Rote Jasminbäume spenden Schatten am Rande des Pools. Die Liege wurde aus einem einzigen Stück Holz gehauen.

EN HAUT, À GAUCHE:
Un bale, *pavillon-salon balinais, met en valeur la piscine carrelée en terrazzo incrusté d'éclats de miroir.*

EN BAS, À GAUCHE:
La roue en bois ancienne accrochée au mur du fond du pavillon est une décoration chargée de sens. Elle provient d'une charrette tirée par des chevaux.

PAGE DE DROITE:
Des frangipaniers dispensent une ombre bienvenue sur le bord de la piscine, là où se trouve une chaise longue taillée dans un bloc de bois.

A VILLA IN SEMINYAK / SEMINYAK

PREVIOUS DOUBLE PAGE LEFT:
The trunks of anaconda-like vines are displayed at the end of a concrete-columned passageway leading from the foyer into the main house.

PREVIOUS DOUBLE PAGE RIGHT:
The front door of intan burlwood with Moroccan handles opens to a foyer corridor revealing old, Indonesian, carved window panels of fine latticework.

LEFT PAGE:
A colonnaded verandah is exposed through an old Balinese door with a patina of aging paint.

RIGHT ABOVE:
Natural wood gives this table a life of its own.

RIGHT BELOW:
An old, brass, four-poster bed from Holland adds elegance to the flowing draperies and gauzy mosquito netting.

VORIGE DOPPELSEITE LINKS:
Geschwungene Baumstämme von anakondagleichen Kletterpflanzen werden am Ende eines Korridors mit Betonsäulen dekorativ zur Schau gestellt.

VORIGE DOPPELSEITE RECHTS:
Die Eingangstür aus Intan-Wurzelholz mit marokkanischen Griffen öffnet sich zu einem Korridor hin und gibt den Blick auf altindonesische geschnitzte Fensterläden mit feinem Gitterwerk frei.

LINKE SEITE:
Durch eine alte balinesische Tür mit der Patina eines in die Jahre gekommenen Anstrichs ist eine Veranda mit Kolonnade zu sehen.

RECHTS OBEN:
Die natürlichen Holzformen und Oberflächen machen aus diesem Tisch fast ein lebendiges Wesen.

RECHTS UNTEN:
Ein altes niederländisches Messinghimmelbett wirkt mit den fließenden Vorhängen und hauchdünnen Moskitonetzen sehr elegant.

PAGE PRÉCÉDENTE, À GAUCHE:
Des troncs-lianes surgissent, tels des anacondas, au fond d'une galerie bordée de colonnes de béton qui relie le vestibule au bâtiment principal.

PAGE PRÉCÉDENTE, À DROITE:
La porte d'entrée en bois d'intan munie de poignées marocaines s'ouvre sur un couloir-vestibule révélant des volets indonésiens à claire-voie finement ouvragés.

PAGE DE GAUCHE :
En poussant une porte balinaise ancienne à la peinture passée, on découvre une véranda bordée de colonnes.

EN HAUT, À DROITE:
Le bois laissé à l'état naturel prête presque vie à cette table.

EN BAS, À DROITE:
Un lit ancien à baldaquin provenant de Hollande donne une certaine élégance aux voilages animés par le vent et à la moustiquaire vaporeuse.

A VILLA IN SEMINYAK / SEMINYAK

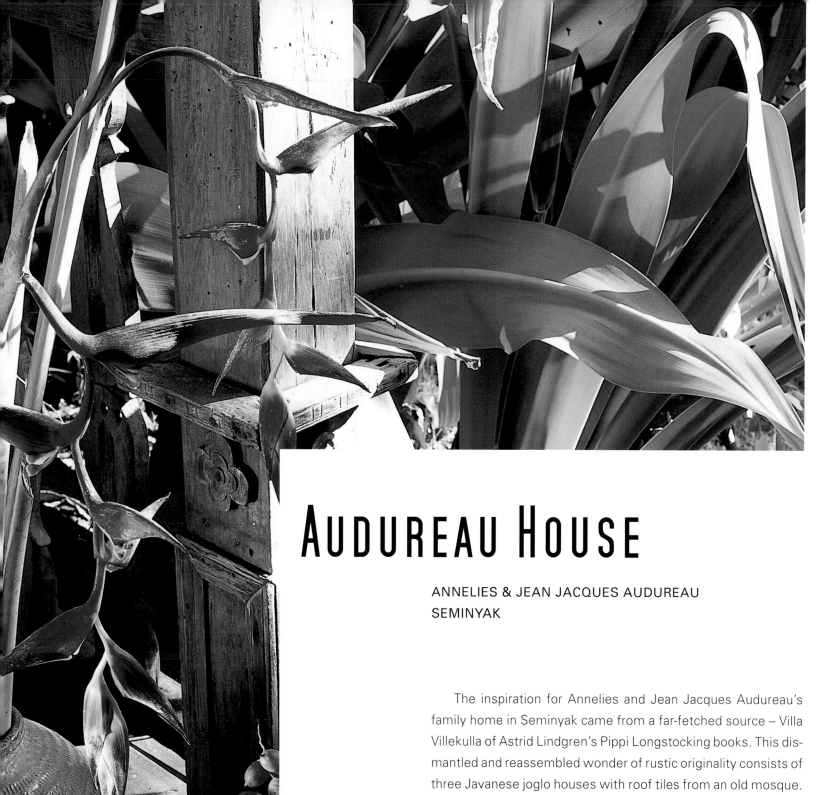

Audureau House

ANNELIES & JEAN JACQUES AUDUREAU
SEMINYAK

The inspiration for Annelies and Jean Jacques Audureau's family home in Seminyak came from a far-fetched source – Villa Villekulla of Astrid Lindgren's Pippi Longstocking books. This dismantled and reassembled wonder of rustic originality consists of three Javanese joglo houses with roof tiles from an old mosque. A courtyard of fruit and palm trees leads to the main house. Its wooden panels and beams have been painted white, while the doors and floors have been left in their natural state. Annelies, an exporter of furnishings, and Jean Jacques, an exporter of pre-fabricated dwellings, collected building materials from Java and artifacts from all over the world before building their Javanese chalet. The faded paint on the shutters, Afghani kilims, big sofas and an antique Chinese medicine chest suggest shabby-chic elegance. Louvered, colonial style doors lead to a verandah with a lattice balustrade, this family gathering place overlooks the tropical garden enveloping this fairy-tale existence.

A colorful arrangement
of hanging heliconia and
natural palm fruit on
the wooden entry porch
welcomes visitors to the
home of the Audureau
family.

Zusammen mit einem
Arrangement natürlicher
Palmfrüchte entbieten
diese hängende Helikoni-
en dem Besucher an der
hölzernen Eingangspforte
zum Haus der Familie Au-
dureau ein farbenfrohes
Willkommen.

Le spectacle coloré d'un
Heliconia collinsiana et
d'un arrangement de
fruits de palmier accueille
les visiteurs sous le porche d'entrée en bois du
domicile des Audureau.

Im Audureau House hätte sich Pippi Langstrumpf wie zu Hause gefühlt – denn Annelies und Jean Jacques Audureau ließen sich von der „Villa Kunterbunt" inspirieren, als sie ihr Domizil entwarfen. Annelies, die Einrichtungsgegenstände nach Europa verkauft, und Jean Jacques, der Fertighäuser exportiert, sammelten jahrelang Kunsthandwerk aus aller Welt, ehe ihr Wunderwerk vollendet war. Jetzt besteht das Anwesen aus drei joglo-Häusern aus Java, die dort auseinander genommen und auf Bali wieder zusammengesetzt wurden. Über einen Hof mit Obstbäumen und Palmen erreicht man das Hauptgebäude – auf seinem Dach leuchten die Ziegel einer alten Moschee in der Sonne, seine Holzbalken strahlen in frischem Weiß, und die Türen sowie Fußböden wurden in ihrem natürlichen Zustand belassen. In den Zimmern sorgen afghanische Wandteppiche, weiche Sofas und eine chinesische Medizintruhe für eine Mischung aus Eleganz und Wohnlichkeit. Lamellentüren im Kolonialstil führen auf die Veranda und in den tropischen Garten.

S'inspirant de la Villa Drôlederepos de Fifi Brindacier, Annelies et Jean Jacques Audureau ont créé une merveille originale et rustique constituée de trois maisons joglo javanaises, démontées puis rassemblées. Les tuiles proviennent d'une mosquée ancienne. Une cour plantée d'arbres fruitiers et de palmiers mène à la maison principale, tout en contrastes avec des panneaux et des poutres peints en blanc et des portes et planchers laissés dans leur état naturel. Annelies, exportatrice de mobilier vers l'Europe, et Jean Jacques, qui exporte des habitations insulaires préfabriquées, ont rassemblé des matériaux de construction provenant de Java et collectionné des objets du monde entier pendant plusieurs années avant de construire leur bungalow javanais. Les couleurs passées des volets peints, les kilims afghans, les canapés profonds et une ancienne armoire à pharmacie chinoise suggèrent une élégance «shabby chic». Des portes à claire-voie de style colonial s'ouvrent sur une véranda et un jardin tropical.

LEFT ABOVE:
A giant Bismarckia nobilis palm, grown from a seedling, towers over the entrance to the main living section of this quaint, old, reassembled joglo house with roof tiles from a Javanese mosque.

LEFT BELOW:
The white concrete walls and floors of the master bedroom are accented by a wooden trunk placed at the foot of the shrouded bed.

RIGHT ABOVE:
The colonial influence is palpable in the louvered wooden doors leading to the verandah with its hand-carved balustrade.

RIGHT BELOW:
The wooden deck of the inviting swimming pool is shaded by an enormous traveler's palm, which evokes an Eastern feeling.

LINKS OBEN:
Eine riesige Bismarckpalme, die hier ursprünglich als Sämling gepflanzt wurde, wacht neben dem Eingang dieses idyllischen wieder aufgebauten joglo-Hauses mit Dachziegeln, die von einer javanischen Moschee stammen.

LINKS UNTEN:
Die Wände und Böden aus Weißbeton werden durch den hölzernen Balken am Fuße des mit Moskitonetz verhüllten Bettes noch stärker betont.

RECHTE SEITE OBEN:
Die hölzernen Lamellentüren führen zur Veranda mit ihrer handgeschnitzten Balustrade, die kolonialen Einfluss verrät.

RECHTE SEITE UNTEN:
Die hölzerne Plattform am einladenden Swimming-Pool liegt im Schatten eines riesigen „Baums der Reisenden", der einen Hauch von Morgenland verbreitet.

EN HAUT, À GAUCHE:
Un gigantesque Bismarckia nobilis cultivé à partir d'une graine domine l'entrée de l'espace de vie principal de cette pittoresque maison joglo ancienne remontée sur place dont les tuiles proviennent d'une mosquée de Java.

EN BAS, À GAUCHE:
Dans la chambre de maîtres, la blancheur des revêtements muraux et du sol en béton est rehaussée par une malle en bois au pied du lit disparaissant sous les voilages.

EN HAUT, À DROITE:
Les portes de bois à claire-voie ouvrant sur la véranda dotée d'une balustrade taillée à la main trahissent une influence coloniale.

EN BAS, À DROITE:
Au bord de la piscine qui invite à la baignade, la plateforme en bois est protégée du soleil par un énorme arbre du voyageur, qui ajoute une touche asiatique à l'ensemble.

AUDUREAU HOUSE / SEMINYAK

An old, wooden, Javanese house in the garden is a classic country setting with rustic furniture and space to store a surfboard for those Bali waves.

Das alte Holzhaus im Garten ist aus Java und im klassischen balinesischen „Country-Stil" eingerichtet, mit rustikalen Möbeln und einem Lagerraum zum Verstauen der Surfbretter, die auf den legendären Wellen von Bali zum Einsatz kommen.

Dans le jardin, cette vieille maison javanaise en bois, qui a quelque chose de très rural avec son mobilier est utilisée pour ranger les planches de surf qui affrontent les vagues de Bali.

AUDUREAU HOUSE / SEMINYAK

VILLA SENJA

CLAUDINE & OLIVIER MESLIN
UMALAS

Stepping into Villa Senja is like entering a French provincial home where Asian influences are blended with North African and Arabian touches and rounded off with Art Deco accents. This tasteful mixture of styles flows together easily against the backdrop of a Balinese rice field, reminding us where we are. French-born Claudine and Olivier Meslin lived in Bali for a decade before building this "chateau." They collected old teak planks, for the floor and ceiling, and massive *joglo*-carved teak beams to support the Javanese style roof shingled with iron-wood. The thick, double walls made of cement have recessed windows with frames and sills of wood. They reflect the French provincial influence, offsetting the European colonial mixture of Art Deco style furniture and Asian pieces highlighted with a subtle Chinese flair. Watching twilight - as "Senja" means – approach from one of the many rattan sofas and chairs on the verandah, one sees shades of purple cast onto the tropical garden and rice fields.

The arched window in the Meslins' bathroom allows ventilation through triangular openings in a geometric terrazzo screen influenced by Islamic designs.

Die offenen Fenster mit ihren islamisch beeinflussten Dreiecksformen im Badezimmer der Meslins sorgen für eine gute Lüftung.

L'aération de la salle de bains des Meslin est assurée par une baie cintrée en terrazzo percée d'ouvertures triangulaires dénotant une influence mauresque.

Wer die Villa Senja betritt, fühlt sich zunächst wie auf einem provenzalischen Landsitz und entdeckt dann immer wieder neue Details aus Asien, Arabien und Nordafrika, die mit Art Déco-Anklängen verbunden werden – jetzt erinnert nur noch der Blick über die Reisfelder daran, dass dieses Haus auf Bali steht. Die französischen Besitzer Claudine und Olivier Meslin lebten bereits ein Jahrzehnt auf der Insel, ehe sie dieses „Château" bauten. Im Lauf der Zeit sammelten sie Teakholzbohlen aus Java, die Böden und Decken schmücken, und massive *joglo*-Teakbalken, die das Schindeldach im javanischen Stil tragen. An die französische Heimat der Hausherren erinnern die dicken Doppelwände aus Beton mit holzgerahmten Türen. In den Räumen verbinden sich Westliches und Fernöstliches – man bewundert kolonial anmutendes Art Déco-Mobiliar und antike Stücke aus China. Während der blauen Stunde zwischen Tag und Nacht ist es auf der Veranda an schönsten, wenn die Dämmerung, das bedeutet „Senja", purpurne Schatten wirft.

En entrant dans la Villa Senja, on a l'impression de pénétrer dans un mas provençal où se marieraient avec bonheur des influences asiatiques, des notes maghrébines et orientales et même une touche d'Art Déco. Les Français Claudine et Olivier Meslin ont vécu à Bali une dizaine d'années avant de construire ce «château». Ils ont pris leur temps pour rassembler une à une les vieilles planches en bois de teck provenant de Java qui ont servi à faire les sols et les plafonds ainsi que les massives poutres en teck sculptées *joglo* qui supportent la toiture de style javanais en bardeaux de bois de fer. L'influence provençale visible dans les épais murs doubles en ciment, dans lesquels ont été encastrés des appuis de fenêtres et des chambranles de portes en bois, contrebalance le style colonial européen mêlant mobilier Art Déco et objets asiatiques. Assis dans un des sofas ou sur une des chaises en rotin de la véranda, on voit le crépuscule – ce que signifie «Senja» – projeter des ombres violettes sur le coquet jardin tropical et les vastes rizières.

24

LEFT ABOVE:
A wooden Chinese screen, set into the wall, frames the Art Deco love seat on the verandah.

LEFT BELOW:
A sublimely casual setting with intricate wicker designs reminiscent of colonial days.

RIGHT ABOVE:
Neo-colonial influences pervade the open verandah sheltered by a nearby pergola of flowering bougainvillea.

RIGHT BELOW:
A Javanese lounging bench overlooks the infinity-edged pool and the terraced rice fields behind an old Javanese house.

FOLLOWING PAGE LEFT:
The French provincial style, stone-floored country kitchen features double walls framed with wooden sills and open cupboards made of polished concrete with basket-woven drawers.

FOLLOWING PAGE RIGHT:
In the shade of freshly cut gardenias, a plate from a leather-bound, nineteenth-century Javanese book displays an example of the architectural style of that era.

LINKS OBEN:
Hinter dem kleinen Art Déco-Rattansofa auf der Veranda sieht man einen hölzernen chinesischen Sichtschutz.

LINKS UNTEN:
Das Flechtwerk der Korbmöbel ruft Erinnerungen an die Kolonialzeit wach.

RECHTE SEITE OBEN:
Auf der offenen Veranda herrschen neokoloniale Einflüsse vor. An die Veranda schließt sich eine Pergola aus blühenden Drillingsblumen an.

RECHTE SEITE UNTEN:
Von der javanischen Liege hat man einen Ausblick auf den scheinbar randlosen Pool und ein altes Java-Haus, das an Reisfeldterrassen angrenzt.

FOLGENDE DOPPELSEITE LINKS:
Mit Steinboden, hölzernen Simsen und offenen Schränken aus poliertem Beton, die mit Körben bestückt sind, orientiert sich diese Landhausküche am provenzalischen Stil aus Frankreich.

FOLGENDE DOPPELSEITE RECHTS:
Im Schatten frisch geschnittener Gardenien zeigt ein in Leder gebundenes javanisches Buch aus dem 19. Jahrhundert Stiche, die Stilrichtungen der einheimischen Baukunst aus der damaligen Zeit darstellen.

EN HAUT, À GAUCHE:
Un panneau ajouré chinois en toile de fond d'une causeuse Art déco en rotin.

EN BAS, À GAUCHE:
Un arrangement d'un naturel exquis d'objets en osier aux motifs complexes rappelle l'époque coloniale.

PAGE DE DROITE, EN HAUT:
Des influences néo-coloniales sont manifestes sur la véranda ouverte. A l'arrière-plan, une pergola sert de support à des bougainvilliers en fleur.

PAGE DE DROITE, EN BAS:
Assis dans cette chaise longue javanaise, on a vue sur la piscine sans bords et sur une vieille maison javanaise à la limite de rizières en terrasses qui s'étendent à perte de vue.

PAGE SUIVANTE, À GAUCHE:
La cuisine rustique au sol de pierre est de style provençal: murs doubles avec appuis de fenêtres en bois et rangements sans portes en béton poli avec des corbeilles tressées en guise de tiroirs.

PAGE SUIVANTE, À DROITE:
Des gardénias fraîchement coupés projettent leur ombre sur un livre javanais du 19e siècle relié cuir qui renferme des gravures représentant les styles architecturaux locaux de l'époque.

28

LEFT:
The antique teak, beam ceilings are influenced by traditional European houses. They are offset by an Asian touch, which includes a Chinese bookcase displaying carved wooden figures from Bali.

RIGHT:
The Art Nouveau style dining area is the family gathering place. Rare wooden carvings of Balinese deities and dancers can be seen on top of the cabinet designed in the style of a Victor Horta replica.

LINKE SEITE:
Die Decken aus antiken Teakholzbalken sind von alten europäischen Häusern beeinflusst. Der chinesische Bücherschrank mit geschnitzten balinesischen Sammelfiguren aus Holz gibt dem Raum dagegen eine asiatische Note.

RECHTE SEITE:
Im Essbereich im Jugendstil versammelt sich die Familie. Über dem Schrank – einer Victor-Horta-Imitation – sieht man seltene holzgeschnitzte balinesische Tänzer und Gottheiten.

PAGE DE GAUCHE:
Les plafonds anciens dotés de poutres en teck témoignent de l'influence des vieilles demeures européennes. Une étagère chinoise accueillant une collection intéressante de figurines balinaises sculptées sur bois apporte une touche asiatique.

PAGE DE DROITE:
La famille se retrouve dans l'espace repas Art nouveau. Ici des sculptures sur bois balinaises d'une grande rareté représentant des divinités et des danseurs surmontent une réplique d'un meuble de Victor Horta.

LEFT ABOVE:
The verandah at the corner of Claudine and Olivier Meslins' master bedroom is a graceful example of romantic style. The hammock has a delicately crocheted border. Displayed below is a wooden mortar of the kind used to pound rice after the harvest.

LEFT BELOW:
A reassembled Javanese house in the garden is at the disposal of guests. Its planks are imbued with the silky patina of 150-year-old teak.

RIGHT:
Both the wooden frame around the entrance to the shower and the soap dish in the terrazzo and concrete bathroom reflect a distinctive Arabian style.

LINKS OBEN:
Die Verandahecke des Schlafzimmers von Claudine und Olivier Meslin wirkt ebenso anmutig wie romantisch mit einer fein umhäkelten Hängematte und einem Holzmörser aus Bali, mit dem nach der Ernte Reis gestampft wurde.

LINKS UNTEN:
Bei dem Gästehaus im Garten handelt es sich um ein wieder aufgebautes Haus aus Java mit einem Boden aus Teakholzbohlen, die über 150 Jahre alt sind und seidig glänzen.

RECHTE SEITE:
Das Bad aus Terrazzo und poliertem Beton ist in unverwechselbaren arabischen Stil gehalten. Der hölzerne Rahmen vom Eingang zur Dusche hat die gleiche Form wie die in der Wand eingelassene Seifenschale.

EN HAUT, À GAUCHE:
La véranda de la chambre de maîtres de Claudine et Olivier Meslin est d'un romantisme exquis avec son hamac agrémenté d'une délicate bordure au crochet et un authentique mortier balinais en bois servant à pilonner le riz après la récolte.

EN BAS, À GAUCHE:
Le pavillon pour les invités dans le jardin est une maison javanaise remontée sur place. Les planches de teck ont acquis leur patine soyeuse au fil de 150 ans.

PAGE DE DROITE:
Dans un angle de la salle de bains en béton et terrazzo, la cabine de douche au chambranle de bois apporte une touche mauresque caractéristique, tout comme le porte-savon encastré.

VILLA SENJA / UMALAS

VILLA MATISSE

CONCHITA KIEN
PANTAI SESEH

While residing for most of the 1980s in a secluded, traditional village in eastern Bali, the Dutch-born Conchita Kien and her mother cultivated a deep understanding of Balinese culture. By the 1990s Conchita had become a jewelry designer and moved closer to the expatriate community living near the beaches of southern Bali. She planned the construction of her first house on a meager budget of $10,000. She pioneered new architectural techniques and reinvented others, creating inspiring designs and changing the future of her own career. Eventually she was even hired to build private villas and spas – such as the famous Bodyworks – was well as boutiques – such as Milo's. In constructing her own new home, Villa Matisse, Conchita employed terrazzo in muted colors with chips of glimmering mother of pearl, for the walls and floors, along with mosaics of broken mirrors and lots of polished silver-gray cement. The ocean side of the two-storied villa has no walls at all.

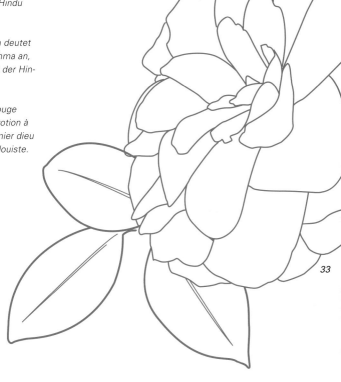

A red umbrella signifying devotion to Brahma, the first god of the Hindu Triad.

Ein roter Schirm deutet Hingabe an Brahma an, den ersten Gott der Hindu-Triade.

Une ombrelle rouge symbole de dévotion à Brahmâ, le premier dieu de la triade hindouiste.

33

Conchita Kien stammt ursprünglich aus den Niederlanden und lebte in den 1980ern acht Jahre lang gemeinsam mit ihrer Mutter in einem traditionellen und abgeschiedenen Dorf im Osten Balis. Dort begann sie, Schmuck zu entwerfen, und zog später an die Südküste der Insel, wo sie mit einem winzigen Startkapital von 10.000 Dollar ihr erstes eigenes Haus entwarf. Mit Mut und Kreativität erfand sie damals völlig neue Techniken, die ihr Gebäude einzigartig machten und ihr zu einer Karriere als Architektin und Designerin verhalfen. Sie wurde für die Gestaltung von Privatvillen auf der Insel engagiert, entwarf das Spa „Bodyworks" und Boutiquen wie „Milo's". Für sich selbst baute Conchita Kien die neue Villa Matisse: Hier verzierte sie die gedeckten Terrazzowände und -böden mit glitzerndem Perlmutt, Spiegelmosaiken und viel silbergrau poliertem Beton. Den Blick in die umliegende Natur und auf den Ozean sollte das Haus nicht stören: Eine Seite der zweistöckigen Villa besitzt keine einzige Wand.

Ayant passé huit ans dans un village traditionnel de l'est de Bali au cours des années 1980, la jeune Hollandaise Conchita Kien et sa mère ont acquis une connaissance profonde de la culture balinaise. Devenue ensuite créatrice de bijoux, Conchita s'est rapprochée de la communauté des expatriés installés près des plages du sud de Bali. Elle a imaginé les plans de sa première maison, avec un budget serré de 10 000 $, lançant et réinventant des techniques et des éléments architecturaux qui ont su séduire. Sa carrière a alors pris un nouveau tournant et on lui a peu à peu confié la construction de villas particulières, de centres thermaux, comme le célèbre Bodyworks, et de boutiques comme Milo's. Pour édifier la Villa Matisse, Conchita a utilisé des techniques comme celle qui consiste à incorporer dans un revêtement de sols et de murs décoratif en terrazzo aux tons fondus des éclats de nacre ou de mosaïques de miroir avec quantité de ciment poli gris argent. Une façade de cette villa à deux étages donnant sur l'océan est dépourvue de murs.

PREVIOUS DOUBLE PAGE LEFT:
An arrangement of Chinese celadon ware harmonizes with the patina of an ancient Shiva lingam.

PREVIOUS DOUBLE PAGE RIGHT:
The riverside guest house features a table and chairs with mosaic patterns made of chipped mirrors. Inspired by Indian crafts.

LEFT ABOVE:
The downstairs sitting area is completely without walls.

LEFT BELOW:
This pillowed sitting area with hout walls exposes a panoramic view of the forest, river and ocean beyond.

RIGHT ABOVE:
An outdoor dining area with a typical Balinese lantern is hidden under a frangipani tree.

RIGHT BELOW:
Monochromatic silver-gray tones of the rich concrete pillars and walls face a minimal courtyard.

VORIGE DOPPELSEITE LINKS:
Das blassgrüne Arrangement aus chinesischen Celadon-Gefäßen harmoniert mit der Patina des antiken Shiva-Lingams.

VORIGE DOPPELSEITE RECHTS:
Im Gästehaus am Fluss findet man einen Tisch und Stühle mit einem Mosaik aus Spiegelsplittern nach indischem Vorbild.

LINKE SEITE OBEN:
Im Wohnbereich des unteren Geschosses fehlen jegliche Wände.

LINKE SEITE UNTEN:
Der wandlose gepolsterte Sitzbereich gibt einen Panoramablick frei auf den Urwald, den Fluss und das Meer dahinter.

RECHTS OBEN:
Ein Essbereich im Freien mit einer typisch balinesischen Laterne liegt verborgen unter einem Roten Jasminbaum.

RECHTS UNTEN:
Monochromatische Silbergrautöne der dicken Betonsäulen und -wände beherrschen den minimalistischen Hof.

DOUBLE PAGE PRÉCÉDENTE, À GAUCHE:
Harmonie parfaite de ces céladons chinois et de la patine d'un lingam ancien.

DOUBLE PAGE PRÉCÉDENTE, À DROITE:
Le pavillon pour les invités en bordure de rivière est agrémenté d'une table et de chaises Revêtus d'une mosaïque déclats de miroir d'inspiration indienne.

PAGE DE GAUCHE, EN HAUT:
La terrasse du bas est entièrement dépourvue de murs.

PAGE DE GAUCHE, EN BAS:
Assis sur des coussins dans l'espace salon ouvert sur l'extérieur, on embrasse du regard la forêt, la vallée et l'océan dans le lointain.

PAGE DE DROITE, EN HAUT:
Le coin repas dans le jardin éclairé par une lanterne typiquement balinaise est dissimulé sous les frangipaniers.

PAGE DE DROITE, EN BAS:
Les camaïeux de gris des élégantes colonnes de béton et des murs font écho à une cour réduite à l'essentiel.

VILLA MATISSE / PANTAI SESEH

LEFT PAGE:
Baby daughter Ruby anxiously waits for lunch in her sturdy antique high chair.

RIGHT PAGE
In a corner of the exposed upper level, a hole in the floor allows a tree to continue to grow.

FOLLOWING DOUBLE PAGE:
Ocean breezes gently blow through the upstairs bedroom, luminous in shades of gray, silver, and white.

LINKE SEITE:
Die kleine Tochter Ruby wartet in ihrem ebenso robusten wie dekorativen Hochstuhl auf ihr Mittagessen.

RECHTE SEITE:
In einer Ecke des oberen Stockwerks mit weißgefärbten Holzböden befindet sich ein Loch, durch das der Baumstamm weiter wachsen kann.

FOLGENDE DOPPELSEITE:
Das Schlafzimmer im oberen Stockwerk wird von einer frischen Meeresbrise durchweht und bildet einen leuchtenden Farbklang aus Grau, Silber und Weiß.

PAGE DE GAUCHE:
Ruby, la fille de Conchita, attend avec impatience son déjeuner, assise dans sa robuste chaise haute ancienne.

PAGE DE DROITE:
Dans un coin de l'étage ouvert, un arbre poursuit sa croissance grâce à un trou ménagé dans le plancher chaulé.

DOUBLE PAGE SUIVANTE:
A l'étage, camaïeu lumineux de gris, argent et blanc dans la chambre rafraîchie par la brise marine.

VILLA MATISSE / PANTAI SESEH

42

LEFT ABOVE:
The clean lines framing the washbasins in the bathroom reflect structural patterns of design found throughout the house.

LEFT BELOW:
The archetypal simplicity of the shower stall's design and the coolness of the polished, white concrete convey a sense of refreshment.

RIGHT ABOVE:
Ruby's nursery is a fairy tale showroom for a little angel.

RIGHT BELOW:
Shocking pink on pink is the flavor of the guest house bedroom overlooking the river.

LINKS OBEN:
Die reduzierten Linien des Waschbeckenbereichs spiegeln die allgemein klaren Strukturen des Hauses wieder.

LINKS UNTEN:
Die Schlichtheit der Duschnische im Bad wirkt mit der Kühle des polierten Weißbetons erfrischend.

RECHTE SEITE OBEN:
Rubys Kinderzimmer ist wie aus einem Märchenbilderbuch für einen kleinen Engel.

RECHTE SEITE UNTEN:
Schockierende Pinktöne geben im Gästeschlafzimmer mit Blick auf den Fluss den Ton an.

EN HAUT, À GAUCHE:
Les lignes épurées du bloc-lavabos se reflètent le design général clair de la maison.

EN BAS, À GAUCHE:
Dans la salle de bains, l'alcôve pour la douche, d'une simplicité exemplaire, véhicule une impression de fraîcheur avec son béton blanc poli.

PAGE DE DROITE, EN HAUT:
La chambre de Ruby semble tout droit sortie d'un conte de fées pour ce petit ange.

PAGE DE DROITE, EN BAS:
Le mariage osé de deux tons de rose donne sa tonalité à la chambre du pavillon réservé aux amis qui donne sur la rivière.

VILLA MATISSE / PANTAI SESEH

The fusion of styles in the living room reflects Conchita's innovative approach; the hand-painted floral patterns on the walls pick up on the dominant theme of deep, sensuous red.

Das Wohnzimmer zeigt jedoch einen gänzlich anderen Stil. Die Wand ist mit Zierblumen handbemalt und endet rundum in einem tiefen, sinnlichen Rot.

Dans le salon de style éclectique, bien que fidèle à la veine créatrice de Conchita, un remarquable revêtement mural peint à la main constitue, avec ses motifs floraux, une toile de fond en harmonie avec les tons de rouge profond et sensuel qui dominent.

44

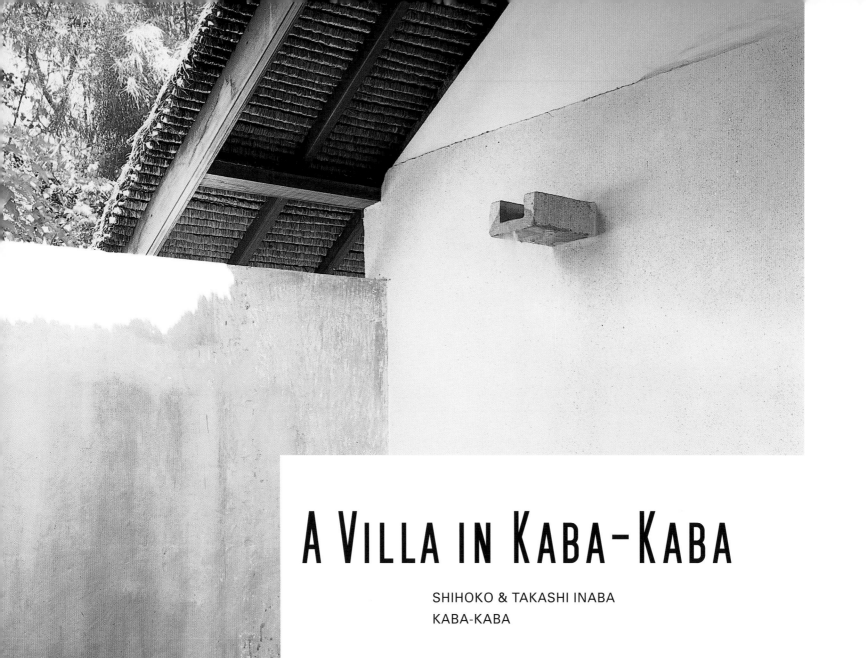

A Villa in Kaba-Kaba

SHIHOKO & TAKASHI INABA
KABA-KABA

In 2000, the Japanese ryokan innkeepers Takashi Inaba and his wife Shihoko moved to Kaba-Kaba, a remote inland village in the district of Tabanan, to be closer to their beloved housekeeper. They also wished to create an open, spacious family home quite unlike their confining living quarters in Shizuoka, Japan. As Takashi-san remarked while sipping a fine, Kyoto-grown tea from a treasured tea bowl, "Europeans begin with the number one. Japanese start, in the mind, with zero. To me, the actual form of an object is more important than its meaning or the system of belief it signifies." True to this philosophy, Takashi created a spacious main house and a separate guest house on sprawling lawns of more than a hectare. Clean lines, white walls, concrete floors and high ceilings are found throughout. As a counterbalance, Takashi re-assembled a small antique teahouse on the edge of the property. It reminds them of the limited space in Japan, but is also an element from the other culture they love so dearly.

A simple shower area of white terrazzo walls with flooring of scattered pebbles and lava stone tiles.

Ein schlichter Duschbereich mit weißen Terrazzowänden und einem Boden aus verstreuten Kieseln und Lavasteinfliesen.

Les murs de terrazzo blanc et les galets et dalles de basalte au sol font de ce coin douche simple.

In ihrer Heimat Japan lebten Takashi Inaba und seine Frau Shihoko in einem kleinen und engen Haus – und sehnten sich immer nach weiten, offenen Räumen. Ihr Traum wurde im Jahr 2000 Wirklichkeit, als sie ins Binnendorf Kaba-Kaba im Südwesten von Bali zogen. Hier schufen sie ein neues Zuhause für ihre Familie – das aber immer noch traditionellen japanischen Philosophien folgt: „Die Europäer fangen mit Eins an. Die Japaner beginnen bei Null", erklärt Takashi. „Für mich ist die eigentliche Form eines Gegenstandes wichtiger als seine Bedeutung oder der Glaube, den er verkörpert." Auf einer mehr als einen Hektar umfassenden Rasenfläche bauten die Inabas ein großzügig gestaltetes Haupthaus und ein separates Gästehaus – beide mit klaren Linien, weißen Wänden, Betonböden und hohen Decken. Am Rand des Grundstück steht noch ein kleines Teehaus, das die Erinnerung an typisch japanische Architektur und ihre räumlichen Einschränkungen wach hält – so hat das Ehepaar das Kunststück fertiggebracht, das Beste aus zwei Kulturen miteinander zu verbinden.

Propriétaires d'une auberge traditionnelle japonaise, Takashi Inaba et son épouse Shihoko ont décidé en l'an 2000 de s'installer dans le district de Tabanan, dans le sud-ouest de l'île. C'est sur le village de Kaba-Kaba, à l'intérieur des terres, qu'ils ont jeté leur dévolu, pour se rapprocher de leur gouvernante bien aimée. Las d'être à l'étroit chez eux au Japon, ils souhaitaient aussi créer une maison spacieuse. Savourant un délicat thé vert dans un précieux bol à thé, Takashi note que pour lui «la forme véritable des objets est plus importante que leur sens ou le système de croyances qu'ils véhiculent.» En accord avec cette philosophie, Takashi a fait ériger sur les pelouses qui s'étendent sur un hectare une vaste maison de maîtres et un pavillon pour les invités, des bâtiments hauts de plafond aux lignes pures, aux murs blancs et aux sols en béton. Takashi a monté une petite maison de thé ancienne à la lisière de la propriété, pour rappeler que l'espace a des limites et pour mêler étroitement les deux cultures si chères au couple.

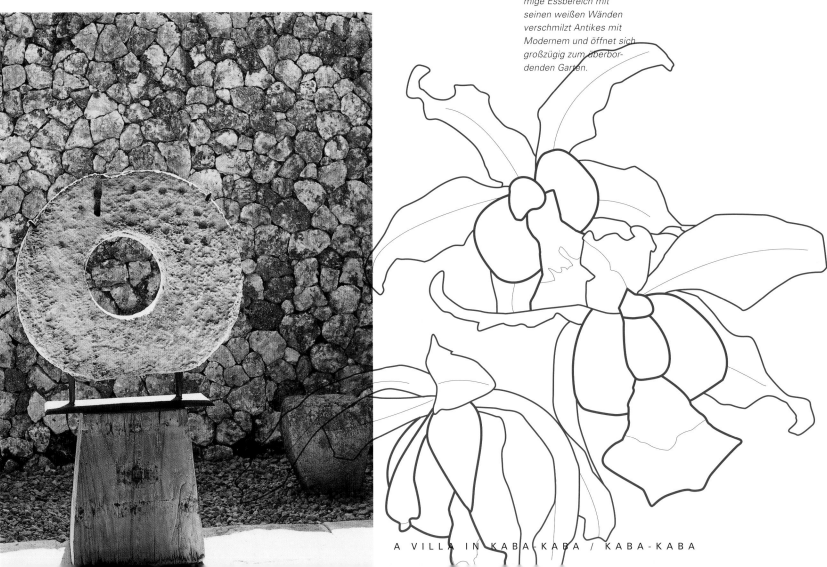

LEFT ABOVE:
Shihoko and her husband, Inaba Takashi enter through the massive teak front doors of their Bali home.

LEFT BELOW:
An antiquated stone cover, once used to keep rats out of a well, has been transformed into a symbolic "zero without limits."

RIGHT ABOVE:
The garden wall made of paras stone mottled with lichen provides a backdrop to the living room, a gallery of timeless antique and primitive furniture.

RIGHT BELOW:
A Dutch colonial daybed is arranged alongside a table of black kafini wood and an aging, primitive, wooden artifact from Kalimantan.

FOLLOWING DOUBLE PAGE:
The airy space of the luminous dining area is defined by white walls and flooring. A fusion of the ancient and the modern, it opens up to the forces residing in the garden.

LINKS OBEN:
Shihoko und ihr Ehemann Takashi Inaba treten durch die massiven Türen aus Teakholz in ihr balinesisches Heim ein.

LINKS UNTEN:
Eine altmodische Steinabdeckung, die einst dazu diente, Ratten aus dem Wasserbrunnen herauszuhalten, verwandelt sich in eine symbolische „Null ohne Grenzen".

RECHTE SEITE OBEN:
Die mit Flechten überzogenen Parassteinwände bilden den Zen-gartenähnlichen Hintergrund des Wohnzimmers, das einer Galerie zeitlosen antiken und primitiven Mobiliars gleicht.

RECHTE SEITE UNTEN:
Ein Tagesbett aus der niederländischen Kolonialzeit und ein niedriger Tisch aus schwarzem Kafiniholz erzeugen zusammen mit einem alternden primitiven Holzartefakt aus Kalimantan eine ruhige Stimmung.

FOLGENDE DOPPELSEITE:
Der helle und geräumige Essbereich mit seinen weißen Wänden verschmilzt Antikes mit Modernem und öffnet sich großzügig zum überbordenden Garten.

EN HAUT, À GAUCHE:
Shikoko Takashi et son mari Inaba sur le seuil de la porte d'entrée en teck massif de leur maison de Bali.

EN BAS, À GAUCHE:
Un couvercle de pierre hors d'âge servant jadis à empêcher les rats d'accéder au puits a été converti en un «zéro infini» symbolique.

PAGE DE DROITE, EN HAUT:
Les murs en pierre de Paras envahis par la mousse ferment le jardin intérieur sur lequel donne le salon, galerie de meubles anciens et primitifs intemporels.

PAGE DE DROITE, EN BAS:
mariage réussi d'un lit de repos colonial hollandais et d'une table basse en bois de kafini noir avec une sculpture primitive de Kalimantan.

DOUBLE PAGE SUIVANTE:
Le coin repas spacieux et lumineux avec ses murs et son sol blancs allie ancien et moderne, face au jardin exubérant.

A VILLA IN KABA-KABA / KABA-KABA

LEFT ABOVE:
A peek into the bedroom – a perfect composition featuring Borneo mats – reflected in a mirror with a carved, wooden frame.

LEFT BELOW:
A bed surrounded by the wooden beams and frame of the lower level of an old rice barn called a lumbung.

RIGHT ABOVE:
Rich simplicity is the result of fusing the ethnic with chic modernism in the living room of the guest house.

RIGHT BELOW:
A fertility symbol, harmonizing with the stone Shiva lingam on the pedestal table, is displayed in the entryway colored by terracotta-tiled floors and Timorese doors.

LINKS OBEN:
Ein Blick in die Komposition des Schlafzimmers, dem Matten aus Borneo und die Reflexionen in einem Spiegel mit geschnitztem Rahmen die perfekte Note verleihen.

LINKS UNTEN:
Ein Bett, das aus den Holzbalken und dem Rahmen einer alten Reisscheune, genannt lumbung, gebaut ist.

RECHTE SEITE OBEN:
Elegante Schlichtheit ist das Ergebnis, wenn sich im Wohnzimmer des Gästehauses ethnische Elemente mit modernem Schick paaren.

RECHTE SEITE UNTEN:
Die Diele erhält Farbe durch die Bodenfliesen aus Terrakotta. Eine Tür aus Timor und ein Fruchtbarkeitssymbol harmonieren mit dem steinernen Shiva-Lingam auf dem Sockeltisch im Foyer.

EN HAUT, À GAUCHE:
aperçu de l'aménagement de la chambre à coucher agrémentée de tapis de Bornéo qui se reflètent dans un miroir au cadre en bois sculpté.

EN BAS, À GAUCHE:
Les montants du baldaquin proviennent du niveau inférieur d'un ancien lumbung, silo à riz balinais.

PAGE DE DROITE, EN HAUT:
La simplicité élégante du salon du pavillon destiné aux invités tient à la fusion des éléments traditionnels et du design moderne.

PAGE DE DROITE, EN BAS:
Dans l'entrée qui doit sa couleur au carrelage de terre cuite, une porte provenant du Timor flanquée d'un symbole de fertilité fait écho au lingam de pierre exposé sur un guéridon dans le vestibule.

52

A VILLA IN KABA-KABA / KABA-KABA

A corner of the living room becomes a primitive enclave with the dark tones of the wooden Sumba cabinet against the white walls.

Eine Ecke des Wohnzimmers wird durch die dunklen Farbtöne des Holzschranks aus Sumba vor den hellen weißen Wänden zu einer urtümlichen Enklave.

Les taintes sombres du bois de armoire Sumba qui contrastent avec les murs d´un blanc lumineux transforment un coin du salon en caverne âge.

54

A VILLA IN KABA-KABA / KABA-KABA

LEFT ABOVE:
The patina of the weathered teak doors framing the entry way to the bedroom.

LEFT BELOW:
Old teak panels behind a primitive wooden chair and a table with handmade paint brushes and a beaded belt from West Papua.

RIGHT ABOVE:
A gallery of forms and wooden shapes of eras past becoming lifestyle art.

RIGHT BELOW:
This unique low bed with mosquito netted high rafters creates the effect of a self-contained room.

LINKS OBEN:
Die Patina verwitterter Türen aus Teakholz bildet den Rahmen zum Eingang ins Schlafzimmer.

LINKS UNTEN:
Eine alte Vertäfelung aus Teakholz bildet den Hintergrund für einen primitiven Holzstuhl und -tisch mit handgefertigten Pinseln und einem Perlengürtel aus West-Papua.

RECHTE SEITE OBEN:
Wie eine Galerie hölzerner Formen aus vergangener Zeit zur Lifestylekunst wird.

RECHTE SEITE UNTEN:
Dieses einzigartige Tiefbett mit seinem mit Moskitonetzen behangenen Sparren vermittelt den Eindruck eines in sich geschlossenen Zimmers.

EN HAUT, À GAUCHE:
Des portes en teck patinées au fil des ans encadrent l'entrée de la chambre.

EN BAS, À GAUCHE:
De vieux panneaux de teck derrieère une chaise et une table en bois d'aspect primitif. Les pinceaux sout faits à la main, la ceinture de perles vient de Papouasie occidentale.

PAGE DE DROITE, EN HAUT:
On dirait une galerie de formes et de volumes en bois des temps passés élevée au rang d'art du style de vie.

PAGE DE DROITE, EN BAS:
Ce lit bas original dans sa cage de chevrons habillée d'une moustiquaire fait l'effet d'une chambre dans la chambre.

56

A VILLA IN KABA-KABA / KABA-KABA

TAMAN SELINI

PEMUTERAN

On the crystal blue northwest coast of Bali, numerous fishing villages can be found along roads lined with tamarind trees. The woody scent of cooking fires flavors the air. A three-hour drive away from crowds of tourists, bars and boutiques, the village of Pemuteran lies on the edge of the hills that make up Bali's largest nature reserve, Bali Barat National Park. The park encompasses 70,000 hectares of wildlife rainforests and 7,000 hectares of coral reefs. The eleven bungalows found in Taman Selini, or "The Garden of the Moon" as it means in English, were built by local villagers and artisans using indigenous materials. Each bungalow features an alfresco shower, a verandah with a traditional four-poster bed and a sitting area perfect for reading a book or taking afternoon tea. The exotic scent lingering in the garden framed by flowering bougainvillea, frangipani, japonica and Hong Kong orchid trees reminds one of the preciousness of this place on the edge of sparkling, clear water.

Details of a door entablature to a bedroom at Taman Selini.

Blicke durch die reich geschnitzte Holztür in eines der Schlafzimmer im Taman Selini.

Détail du chambranle d'une porte à Taman Selini et vue dans la chambre à coucher.

An der Nordwestküste von Bali, drei Autostunden vom Touristentrubel entfernt, liegen kleine Fischerdörfer mit Tamarindenalleen – hier verbindet sich der holzige Duft mit der leicht salzigen Meeresbrise und den würzigen Schwaden der Herdfeuer. Eines dieser Dörfer ist Pemuteran, das an das größte Naturreservat der Insel grenzt – den Bali Barat Nationalpark, zu dem 70.000 Hektar Regenwald und 7.000 Hektar Korallenriff gehören. Hier wohnt man an schönsten in einem der elf Bungalows von Taman Selini, was übersetzt „Der Garten des Mondes" bedeutet. Die zauberhaften Häuser wurden von Dorfbewohnern und einheimischen Handwerkern mit ortsüblichen Materialien erbaut und besitzen den ganzen Charme des ländlichen Bali. Zu jedem Bungalow gehören eine Außendusche und eine Veranda mit Himmelbett und Sitzecke – wie geschaffen zum Schmökern oder Teetrinken am Nachmittag. Und wenn vom Garten der zarte Duft von Bougainvillea, Rotem Jasmin und Japanischer Quitte herüberzieht, weiß man, dass man es gefunden hat: das kleine Stück vom Paradies.

Le littoral d'un bleu cristallin du nord-ouest de Bali est ponctué de villages de pêcheurs. Dans leurs rues bordées de tamarins, les cuisinières au feu de bois répandent un parfum agréable. A trois heures de voiture des hordes de touristes, des bars et des commerces, le village de Pemuteran se trouve à la lisière des lointaines collines du parc national de Bali Barat, qui s'étend sur 70 000 hectares de forêt vierge abritant une faune sauvage ainsi que sur 7 000 hectares de récifs de coraux. Les onze bungalows de Taman Selini, «Le Jardin de la Lune», ont été construits dans des matériaux de la région par des habitants et des artisans du village. Chaque bungalow est pourvu d'une douche et, en façade, d'une véranda meublée du traditionnel lit à baldaquin dans lequel il fait bon lire ou prendre le thé de l'après-midi. Dans le jardin, des bougainvilliers, des frangipaniers, des cognassiers du Japon et des arbres à orchidées (bauhimia) exhalant des senteurs exotiques rappellent à l'invité de passage la magie de cet endroit.

PREVIOUS DOUBLE PAGE LEFT:
Each bungalow opens to a tastefully decorated private verandah.

PREVIOUS DOUBLE PAGE RIGHT:
The verandah's daybed is in the traditional Balinese style.

LEFT ABOVE:
The hospitality of the Taman Selini staff extends to serving meals right on the beach.

LEFT BELOW:
Breakfast is served with luscious tropical fruits and decorative flowers.

RIGHT ABOVE:
The bluest of waters and a multitude of colorful fish make for ideal boating, adventuresome diving and fascinating snorkeling.

RIGHT BELOW:
The shady verandah is both a living area and an extension of the garden.

VORIGE DOPPELSEITE LINKS:
Jeder Bungalow öffnet sich zu einer geschmackvoll dekorierten privaten Veranda hin.

VORIGE DOPPELSEITE RECHTS:
Das Tagesbett der Veranda ist im traditionellen balinesischen Stil gehalten.

LINKS OBEN:
Zur Gastfreundschaft des Personals von Taman Selini gehört es auch, dass Mahlzeiten unmittelbar am Strand serviert werden.

LINKS UNTEN:
Das Frühstück wird mit schmackhaften Tropenfrüchten und dekorativen Blumen serviert.

RECHTE SEITE OBEN:
Das tiefblaue Wasser mit einer Unzahl bunter Fische empfiehlt sich für einen abenteuerlichen Tauch- oder Schnorchelausflug mit dem Boot.

RECHTE SEITE UNTEN:
Die schattige Veranda ist sowohl Teil des Wohnbereichs als auch eine Erweiterung des Gartens.

PAGE PRÉCÉDENTE, À GAUCHE:
Chaque bungalow donne sur une véranda particulière décorée avec goût.

PAGE PRÉCÉDENTE, À DROITE:
lit de repos traditionnel balinais dans la véranda.

EN HAUT, À GAUCHE:
Le personnel de Taman Selini va jusqu'à servir des repas directement sur la plage.

EN BAS, À GAUCHE:
fruits succulents et fleurs multicolores sur la table du petit-déjeuner.

PAGE DE DROITE, EN HAUT:
Les eaux d'un bleu déncre se prêtent à la plongée sous-marine ou, avec masque et tuba, à la découverte de poissons aux vives couleurs.

PAGE DE DROITE, EN BAS:
La véranda ombragée qui tient lieu de salon est un prolongement du jardin.

TAMAN SELINI / PEMUTERAN

PANCHORAN ESTATE

LINDA GARLAND
UBUD

Everything Linda Garland touches becomes magical. The internationally acclaimed Irish designer and doctor of philosophy has also bewitched such eclectic admirers as Mick Jagger, Donna Karan, Richard Branson and Bono, convincing them to experience this spellbinding 20-acre domain called Panchoran. To the south of Ubud, in the village of Nyuh Kuning, it is nestled in a river valley surrounded by ravishing mountains forested with specimen bamboo plants. There Garland conjures up designs endorsed by Architectural Digest, making her one of the world's top 50 designers. Her designs ranging from bamboo furniture through to home furnishings have continued to evolve through out the three decades she has been living in Bali. Her prolific work on developing bamboo as a renewable forest resource, and promoting its many uses, earned her the Upakati Award, Indonesia's highest national honor. Garland continues to build more romantic houses and poetic bungalows secluded in the botanical splendor of her estate.

67

A shower, alfresco, refreshes the lush ferns while a terracotta pot and coconut shell ladle are offered for traditional style "mandi" bathing.

Eine Dusche im Freien erfrischt auch die üppigen Farne, während ein riesiges Terrakottagefäß und eine Schöpfkelle aus einer Kokosnussschale für ein Bad im traditionellen mandi-Stil zur Verfügung stehen.

Une douche en plein air rafraîchit les fougères exubérants tandis qu'une jarre en terre cuite et une louche faite de l'écorce d'une noix de coco sont mises à disposition pour le mandi, le bain traditionnel.

Die Gästeliste von Panchoran Estate liest sich wie ein who is who des internationalen Showbiz, der Wirtschaft und Politik: Hier ließen sich schon Stars wie Mick Jagger, Bono, Donna Karan und Richard Branson von der Magie Balis verzaubern. Herrin über das acht Hektar große Gut in Nyhu Kuning südlich von Ubud ist Linda Garland – promovierte irische Designerin und laut Architectural Digest eine der 50 besten Designerinnen der Welt. Sie setzt vor allem auf Bambus als umweltfreundliches, erneuerbares und holzfreies Material, das ungezählte Bauvarianten zulässt – für dieses Engagement erhielt sie sogar den Upakati Award, die höchste Ehrung der Republik Indonesien für Verdienste um das Land. Linda Garland lässt sich jeden Tag von Panchoran Estate und den majestätischen, dicht bewaldeten Bergen im Hintergrund inspirieren – das Anwesen wird beständig um romantisch-charmante Privathäuser und Bungalows mit fast poetischem Flair erweitert.

Styliste de renommée internationale et docteur en philosophie, Linda Garland a ensorcelé des personnalités aussi différentes que Mick Jagger, Donna Karan, Richard Branson et Bono, les amenant à vivre l'expérience de Panchoran, une résidence enchanteresse construite sur une propriété d'une dizaine d'hectares. C'est au sud d'Ubud, dans le village de Nyuh Kuning, au bord d'une rivière encastrée dans des montagnes majestueses couvertes de forêts de bambous que Linda Garland fait apparaître des créations que la revue Architectural Digest a saluées, classant cette femme parmi les 50 plus grands designers du monde. Ses travaux intensifs visant à faire du bambou une alternative écologique au bois ainsi que sur les innombrables utilisations de ce matériau par la population, lui ont valu le Upakati Award, la plus haute distinction décernée pour services rendus à la nation indonésienne. Dans la propriété agrandie parcelle par parcelle, on découvre des bungalows et maisons particulières poétiques le long de sentiers sinuant à travers une végétation luxuriante.

68

LEFT ABOVE:
Smooth river rocks are embedded in the stairways leading to the three-tiered wantilan style main house of the Garland Estate.

LEFT BELOW:
Walls woven of flattened bamboo branches offset the natural earth tones of the assorted old terracotta pots.

RIGHT ABOVE:
The first sight when entering the gates of Panchoran is of the long, connected, main house with its alang-alang thatched roofs.

RIGHT BELOW:
Linda Garland's trademark bamboo sofas embellish the wooden verandah, as seen in a view from the living room overlooking the sloping lawns, the river gorge and the jungle on her property.

FOLLOWING PAGE LEFT:
In one of the many sitting pavilions, a black bamboo tray provides a contrast to crisp white linens with white embroidery.

FOLLOWING PAGE RIGHT:
A capricious, thatch-roofed pavilion that Linda calls the "Jungle Gym" has been skillfully constructed to span the banks of the river that flows underneath it.

LINKS OBEN:
Glatt geschmirgelter Flusskies wurde in dem Boden der Treppe verarbeitet, die zu dem im wantilan-Stil gebauten dreistöckigen Hauptgebäude des Garland-Besitzes führt.

LINKS UNTEN:
Aus geplätteten Bambuszweigen geflochtene Wände harmonieren mit den natürlichen Erdtönen der diversen Terrakottatöpfe.

RECHTE SEITE OBEN:
Eine Ansicht der verschiedenen, miteinander verbundenen und mit alang-alang gedeckten Dachstrukturen des Hauptgebäudes gibt einen der ersten Eindrücke beim Betreten von Panchoran wieder.

RECHTE SEITE UNTEN:
Auf der Veranda mit ihrem Holzboden vor dem Wohnzimmer sieht man Linda Garlands charakteristische Bambussofas. Der davor gelegene Rasen fällt steil zur Schlucht des Flusses und zum riesigen Dschungel jenseits ihres Grundstücks hin ab.

FOLGENDE DOPPELSEITE LINKS:
In einem der vielen Sitzpavillons bildet ein schwarzes Bambustablett einen Kontrast zum blendenden Weiß der Laken und Stoffe.

FOLGENDE DOPPELSEITE RECHTS:
Ein spektakuläres, mit einem Grasdach gedecktes Haus wurde geschickt als Spannkonstruktion über den darunter liegenden Fluss gebaut.

EN HAUT, À GAUCHE:
Des galets lisses ont été incrustés dans le sol de l'escalier qui mène au bâtiment principal de la propriété dans le style wantilan.

EN BAS, À GAUCHE:
Des cloisons de lattes de bambou tressées font écho aux tons ocre naturels des diverses jarres en terre cuite.

PAGE DE DROITE, EN HAUT:
Les constructions allongées coiffées de chaume d'alang alang qui constituent la maison principale sont ce que l'on aperçoit en premier en entrant à Panchoran.

PAGE DE DROITE, EN BAS:
Les sofas en bambou signés Linda Garland, agrémentent la véranda dotée d'un plancher dans le prolongement du salon. La pelouse située devant descend à pic vers la gorge creusée par la rivière et vers la vaste jungle, audelà de sa propriété.

PAGE SUIVANTE À GAUCHE:
Dans l'un des nombreux pavillons où il fait bon s'asseoir, un plateau de bambou noir tranche sur les impeccables textiles brodés blanc sur blanc.

PAGE SUIVANTE A DROITE:
«Jungle Gym», comme Linda Garland appelle cette folie coiffée d'un toit de chaume, d'un charme aérien spectaculaire, a été construite avec habileté au-dessus de la rivière.

PREVIOUS DOUBLE PAGE LEFT:
The water of a 25-meter swimming pool reflects a bale sitting pavilion set amid verdant foliage.

PREVIOUS DOUBLE PAGE RIGHT ABOVE:
The Coconut House, one of several scattered guest houses overlooks a bamboo forest.

PREVIOUS DOUBLE PAGE RIGHT BELOW:
The interior of a guest house bedroom decorated in a symphony of white on white and accented by welcoming plantation chairs.

LEFT:
Leftover bamboo chips are used to create textured flooring and a decorative bedside table.

RIGHT ABOVE:
The River House exudes classic English colonial ambience with many comfortable pieces of Garland furniture and carved wooden panels on the walls.

RIGHT BELOW:
A detail of the delicately carved wall panels in the Kudus style from East Java.

VORHERIGE SEITE LINKS:
Inmitten üppigen Laubwerks spiegelt sich ein bale-Sitzpavillon in einem Pool mit 25-Meter-Bahnen.

VORHERIGE SEITE RECHTS OBEN:
Das Coconut House ist eines von mehreren auf dem Grundstück verstreuten Gästehäusern.

VORHERIGE SEITE RECHTS UNTEN:
Einladende Pflanzerstühle im Kolonialstil setzen einen Akzent im Schlafzimmer eines der Gästehäuser, in dem sonst weiße Farbtöne symphonisch aufeinander abgestimmt sind.

LINKE SEITE:
Übrig gebliebene Bambusspäne finden neue Verwendung als Belag für den Fußboden und den dekorativen Nachttisch.

RECHTS OBEN:
Das River House zeichnet sich durch seinen klassischen englischen Kolonialstil mit bequemen Möbelstücken nach Entwürfen von Linda Garland und reich geschnitzten Holzvertäfelungen aus.

RECHTS UNTEN:
Ein Ausschnitt aus den fein geschnitzten Wandvertäfelungen im Kudus-Stil Ostjavas.

PAGE PRÉCÉDENTE, À GAUCHE:
Un bale, pavillon ouvert tenant lieu de salon, se reflète dans un bassin de 25 mètres de long.

PPAGE PRÉCÉDENTE, À DROITE, EN HAUT:
La Coconut House, l'une des villas disséminées sur la propriété, surplombe une forêt de bambous.

PPAGE PRÉCÉDENTE, À DROITE, EN BAS:
La symphonie de blanc dans cette chambre est soulignée par des chaises de style colonial invitant à la détente.

PAGE DE GAUCHE:
Des copeaux de bambou de récupération ont trouvé des utilisations nouvelles: sols à la texture intéressante et ravissante table de chevet.

EN HAUT, À DROITE:
dans la River House, aménagement colonial britannique classique caractérisé par du mobilier confortable Garland et des murs lambrissés de panneaux sculptés.

EN BAS, À DROITE:
détail des panneaux muraux délicatement sculptés dans le style kudu de l'est de Java.

PANCHORAN ESTATE / UBUD

Begawan Giri Estate

UBUD

The Begawan Giri Estate caters to those who value both the sophisticated and the natural on a high level of excellence. Its exclusive privacy muffles all but the most ephemeral rumors concerning the many celebrities – including Donna Karan, Sting, Bono and Susan Sarandon – who have resided in these luxurious residences, surrounded by mountain mists. Set on 22 acres of landscaped tropical parkland, its original owner, the British entrepreneur Bradly Gardner, started a nine-year process of evolution. The architect Cheong Yew Kuan envisioned five private residences, each special and singular in its design. They were intended to represent the various cultures in the Indonesian region as well as the five natural elements. This vision took on an exceptional form in becoming reality along the dramatic Ayung River gorge, in a secluded, traditional Balinese village north of Ubud.

*The lava stone gateway
leads to a path descend-
ing 200 steps to the spa
called, "The Source".*

*Durch das Tor aus Lava-
gestein betritt man einen
Pfad, der 200 Stufen
hinab zu dem Spa, „The
Source" genannt, führt.*

*Une fois passé ce portail
en basalte, le visiteur
descend 200 marches
jusqu'au spa appelé «The
Source».*

Willkommen in einer anderen Welt: Begawan Giri Estate eröffnet seinen Gästen ein Märchenreich voller Luxus, Exklusivität und Privatsphäre pur. Die Hotelresidenzen liegen so weit abseits jeglichen Alltags und sind so gut geschützt, dass sogar VIPs hier ungestörte Tage verbringen können – die Nachricht von prominenten Besuchern wie Sting oder Susan Sarandon bleibt stets nur ein Gerücht. Geschaffen hat dieses einzigartige Hideaway der britische Unternehmer Bradley Garner – er ließ das mehr als neun Hektar große Gelände innerhalb von neun Jahren aus dem balinesischen Dschungel herauswachsen. Sein Architekt Cheong Yew Kuan entwarf fünf luxuriöse Häuser, die stellvertretend für die verschiedenen Kulturen Indonesiens und die Elemente der Natur stehen. Sie sind mit einheimischem Holz, Steinen aus Sumba und Seidenstoffen aus Thailand eingerichtet und eröffnen eine unvergessliche Sicht über den Fluss Ayung. Auch das Spa und das Restaurant machen wunschlos glücklich – wie es sich im Märchen eben gehört.

Il émane de Begawan Giri Estate un mélange de sophistication et de naturel, qui comble au-delà de leurs espérances les amateurs d'excellence. La discrétion de mise en ces lieux est si grande que le séjour de célébrités, telles que Donna Karan, Sting, Bono et Susan Sarandon, dans ces luxueuses résidences perdues dans les brumes des montagnes tient de la rumeur. C'est un parc paysager tropical d'une dizaine d'hectares que le propriétaire d'origine, l'entrepreneur britannique Bradley Gardner, a fait naître de la jungle en l'espace de neuf ans. L'architecte Cheong Yew Kuan a imaginé cinq résidences privées, chacune d'une grande originalité. Elles représentent les différentes cultures régionales de l'Indonésie ainsi que les cinq éléments naturels. Et cette vision s'est faite réalité dans un village traditionnel balinais retiré au nord d'Ubud, avec une vue imprenable sur les gorges de la rivière Ayung.

82

PREVIOUS DOUBLE PAGE:
Tirta-Ening Villa (Clear Water), where Sting stayed, boasts an infinity-edged private swimming pool hanging over a tropical forest.

LEFT ABOVE:
This roofed, Padurakas style gateway made of paras stone leads to the villa called Wanakasa, which means "Forest in the Mist."

LEFT BELOW:
A candi terracotta (small replica of a temple), in the style of Javanese royalty of the Majaphit era and the Sriwijaya Kingdom, stands in the middle of the pool that belongs to the villa called Umabona, "House of the Earth Son."

RIGHT ABOVE:
Begawan Giri's terraced water garden next to the spa is full of ponds with shrimp and fish raised for culinary delights prepared in the restaurant kitchens.

RIGHT BELOW:
Wanakasa's living area is built around a banyan tree that is intertwined with a frangipani tree, thereby creating a single holy tree.

VORHERGEHENDE DOPPEL-SEITE:
Die Villa namens Tirta-Ening („Klares Wasser"), wo schon der prominente Sänger und Schauspieler Sting wohnte, verfügt über einen vermeintlich randlosen Swimming-Pool, der über dem Tropenwald zu schweben scheint.

LINKS OBEN:
Der überdachte Eingang aus Parasstein im Paduraksa-Stil führt zur Villa Wanakasa, was so viel bedeutet wie „Wald im Nebel".

LINKS UNTEN:
Mitten im Pool der Villa Umabona („Haus des Erdensohns") steht eine Candi-Terrakotte im Stil des javanischen Königshauses aus der Majaphit-Ära und der Epoche des Sriwijaya-Königreichs.

RECHTE SEITE OBEN:
Der terrassenförmigen Wassergarten von Begawan Giri neben dem Spa besteht aus zahlreichen Teichen mit Garnelen und Fischen, die man hier züchtet, um sie in den Restaurantküchen zu kulinarischen Genüssen zuzubereiten.

RECHTE SEITE UNTEN:
Der Wohnbereich von Wanakasa ist um einen Affenbrotbaum gebaut, der mit einem Roten Jasmin verwachsen ist und damit einen einzigen heiligen Baum bildet.

DOUBLE PAGE PRÉCÉDENTE:
Une piscine privée sans bords surplombant la forêt tropicale fait la fierté de la villa Tirta-ening («Eau Claire»), dans laquelle le célèbre chanteur et acteur Sting a séjourné.

EN HAUT, À GAUCHE:
Cette entrée couverte, construite en pierre de Paras dans le style paduraksa, mène à la villa Wanakasa («Forêt dans les brumes»).

EN BAS, À GAUCHE:
Au centre de la piscine de la villa Umabona («Maison du fils de la Terre ») s'élève un candi en terre cuite, réplique miniature d'un temple dans le style royal javanais à l'époque Majaphit et à celle du royaume Sriwijaya.

EN HAUT, À DROITE:
Dans les bassins du jardin d'eau en terrasses qui jouxte le spa évoluent des crevettes et des poissons d'élevage qui serviront à préparer es merveilles culinaires qui sortent des cuisines du restaurant.

EN BAS, À DROITE:
Les pièces de sejour de la villa Wanakasa sont construites autour d'un figuier banian et d'un frangipanier enlacés en un arbre sacré.

LEFT ABOVE:
Three tons of rock, including a hewn-stone basin, contribute to the exotic setting for bathing at the Clear Water Villa.

LEFT BELOW:
Rose petals strewn in the circular, terrazzo bathtub, built into the ironwood deck of "The Source" spa, extend an invitation to be pampered. The spa was voted the "Best Overseas Hotel Spa" in the world.

RIGHT ABOVE:
Surrounded by mossy walls and stairways, the Holy Springs of the resort are made accessible to the local villagers.

RIGHT BELOW:
Locally produced ceramic crockery is featured at meals and tea time.

LINKE SEITE OBEN:
Drei Tonnen Felsbrocken und eine aus einem Fels gehauene Badewanne schaffen eine exotische, dabei natürliche Umgebung für das Bad in der Villa des „klaren Wassers".

LINKE SEITE UNTEN:
Rosenblütenblätter wurden in die runde Wanne aus Terrazzo gestreut. Die auf den Eisenholzböden stehenden Liegen im Spa „The Source" laden zu einem unübertrefflichen Verwöhnerlebnis ein. Das Begawan Giri wurde in Großbritannien als „bestes ausländisches Hotel-Spa" der Welt ausgezeichnet.

RECHTS OBEN:
Die heilige Quelle in der Anlage, umgeben von moosbewachsenen Wänden und Treppen, wurde für die Einheimischen aus dem Dorf zugänglich gemacht.

RECHTS UNTEN:
Keramikgeschirrgut aus einheimischer Produktion kommt zu den Mahlzeiten und zur „Tea Time" auf den Tisch.

EN HAUT, À GAUCHE:
Avec cette baignoire taillée dans un bloc de pierre pesant trois tonnes, nature et exotisme sont au rendez-vous pour le bain à la villa «Eau Claire».

EN BAS, À GAUCHE:
Des pétales de rose flottant à la surface d'une baignoire ronde en terrazzo reposant sur la terrasse en bois de fer du spa «La Source» invitent à une séance de détente inoubliable. Le Begawan Giri été élu en Grande-Bretagne meilleur hôtel-spa d'outre-mer au monde.

EN HAUT, À DROITE:
Entourées de murs et d'escaliers recouverts de mousse, les sources sacrées de l'établissement thermal sont accessibles aux habitants du village.

EN BAS, À DROITE:
De la vaisselle en faïence produite sur place est à l'honneur à l'heure des repas et du thé.

BEGAWAN GIRI ESTATE / UBUD

LEFT ABOVE:
The tree trunks hollowed out to accommodate washbasins at the Tejasuara ("Sound of Fire") residence exude a kind of primitive elegance with tribal overtones.

LEFT BELOW:
The palimanan, limestone fascia, used in the shower area contrast strikingly with the warm tone of the merbau wood on the walls of the bathroom.

RIGHT ABOVE:
The sophisticated yet boldly primeval ambience of the Tejasurara residence has roots in the island of Sumba, from whence 1,200 tons of stone were imported. Other elements include recycled telegraph poles and a fire pit at the edge of the pool.

RIGHT BELOW:
The slats of merbau wood used to weave the wall coverings highlight the black bamboo bed and the roughly hewn Javanese bench in the bedroom of the villa.

LINKS OBEN:
Die ausgehöhlten Baumstämme mit eingesetzten Waschbecken in der Villa Tejasurara („Klang des Feuers") strahlen eine ursprüngliche Eleganz mit ethnischer Note aus.

LINKS UNTEN:
Der Duschbereich aus Palimanan, einem Kalkstein, steht in eindrucksvollem Kontrast zu den Badezimmerwänden aus warmem Merbauholz.

RECHTE SEITE OBEN:
Das raffinierte, dabei archaische Aussehen der Villa Tejasurara hat seine Ursprünge auf der Insel Sumba, von der 1.200 Tonnen Gestein ebenso importiert wurden wie die Massivholzsäulen aus wiederverwerteten Telegrafenmasten.

RECHTE SEITE UNTEN:
Die Holzwand aus einem Merbaulattengeflecht akzentuiert das schwarze Bambusbett und die grob behauene javanische Sitzbank im Schlafzimmer der Villa Tejasuara.

EN HAUT, À GAUCHE:
Les troncs évidés dans lesquels des vasques ont été encastrées donnent à la villa Tejasuara («Bruit du feu») un parfum d'élégance primitive avec des notes tribales et ethniques.

EN BAS, À GAUCHE:
Le calcaire de Palimanan choisi comme revêtement pour le coin douche, offre un contraste saisissant avec la chaleur du bois de merbau des murs de la salle de bains.

EN HAUT, À DROITE:
L'atmosphère tout à la fois raffinée et audacieusement primitive de la villa Tajasurara tient aux 1 200 tonnes de pierre et aux poteaux télégraphiques de récupération en guise de massives colonnes en bois importés de l'île de Sumba.

EN BAS, À DROITE:
Dans la chambre de la villa, le treillis de merbau au mur met en valeur le lit de bambou noir et le banc javanais d'une facture rustique.

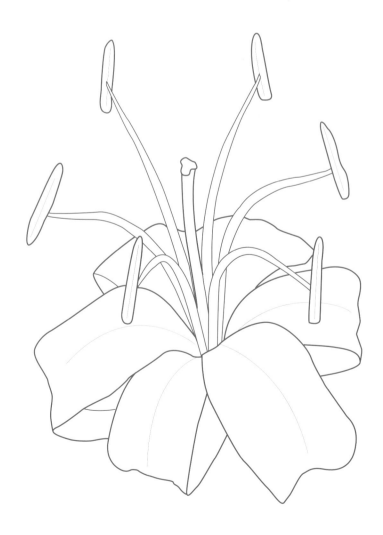

BEGAWAN GIRI ESTATE / UBUD

LEFT:

The cuisine is authentic and uses ingredients from the estate's organic vege-table garden as well as its poultry, fish and prawn farms.

RIGHT:

The "Kudus House" res-taurant is a third-genera-tion Javanese house with exceptionally exquisite carved wooden panels and antique tiled floors.

LINKE SEITE:

Das Essen wird zubereitet mit Geflügel, Fisch und Garnelen aus eigener Züchtung und Bio-Gemüse aus dem eigenen Garten.

RECHTE SEITE:

Das „Kudus House" ge-nannte Restaurant ist ein ursprünglich javanisches Haus aus dem Besitz einer dritten Familienge-neration mit einer beson-ders außergewöhnlichen Vertäfelung aus erlesenen, geschnitzten Hölzern und einem Fußboden aus anti-ken Fliesen.

PAGE DE GAUCHE:

Le chef n'utilise que des volailles, poissons, crevettes et légumes bio élevés ou produits sur la propriété.

PAGE DE DROITE :

Le restaurant Kudus Hou-se, établissement javanais depuis trois générations, s'enorgueillit de panneaux de bois délicatement sculptés et de carrelages anciens au sol.

88

Cynthia & John Hardy

UBUD

John and Cynthia Hardy asked the Malaysian-born architect Cheong Yew Kuan to help realize their fantasy of living in trees. It led him to create an architectural hybrid, a traditional Borneo longhouse high above the Ayung River in Ubud. John, came from Canada in 1975. In the late 1980s he and his Californian wife Cynthia launched a jewelry business that skyrocketed and became internationally renowned. They added a line of art objects. The house evolved slowly from a tent, to a failed barn, to the image of a house far above the ground. It ultimately became the timber longhouse they now call home. The lower story has no walls and is supported by used, ironwood, electrical poles and roughly hewn beams. The high, tea tree ceilings, passageways of woven and plastered bamboo, and folding windows in the upper story allow the sounds of the river to be carried in on the breezes from the rice fields. The Hardy philosophy of "sustainable luxury" is vooted in the flourishing organic gardens.

Visitors to the Hardy Estate are welcomed by a bamboo bridge leading over a fishpond to stone pathways along the edge of a miniature bamboo forest.

Eine Bambusbrücke, die einen Fischteich überbrückt, und steinerne Gehwege, die an einem Miniaturbambuswald vorbeiführen, heißen Besucher auf dem Gelände der Hardys willkommen.

Un pont de bambou enjambant un bassin à poissons et des sentiers de pierre bordant une forêt de bambous miniature accueillent le visiteur à l'entrée de la propriété des Hardy.

Mitten in den Baumkronen zu leben und gleichsam über der Erde zu schweben – das war schon lange ein Wunsch von John und Cynthia Hardy, die gemeinsam eine international renommierte Marke für Schmuck und Kunstobjekte aufgebaut haben. Der aus Malaysia stammende Architekt Cheong Yew Kuan ließ ihren Traum Wirklichkeit werden: Inspiriert von den traditionellen Pfahlbauten Borneos entwarf er ein „Langhaus" hoch über dem Fluss Ayung bei Ubud, in dem der Kanadier John und die Amerikanerin Cynthia ihren perfekten Lebensraum gefunden haben. Das Untergeschoss, das ganz ohne Wände auskommt, wird von ausrangierten Strommasten aus Eisenholz sowie grob bearbeiteten Holzbalken getragen. Dank der hohen Decken aus Teebaumholz und der Klappfenster im Obergeschoss weht immer eine frische Brise durch die Räume – und wo immer man sich aufhält, hört man das leise Rauschen des Flusses und blickt weit über die Reisfelder.

John et Cynthia Hardy rêvaient de vivre dans les arbres et l'architecte d'origine malaise Cheong Yew Kuan a recréé, au-dessus de la rivière Ayung, un hybride architectural d'une ferme traditionnelle sur pilotis de Bornéo. Le Canadien John Hardy s'est installé à Bali en 1975 et, à la fin des années 1980, avec sa femme Cynthia, d'origine californienne, il avait lancé ce qui est aujourd'hui une marque de bijoux et d'objets d'art connue dans le monde entier. La construction d'un foyer s'est faite en plusieurs étapes : vie sous la tente pendant quelques années, construction d'une grange qui s'est soldée par un échec, jusqu'à ce que s'élève leur maison actuelle, une construction allongée à structure en bois qui s'intègre parfaitement dans l'environnement. Le rez-de-chaussée repose sur des poteaux électriques de récupération en bois de fer et des poutres taillées à la main. Avec ses plafonds hauts en bois de théier, il est ouvert aux brises, à la vue sur les rizières et au murmure de la rivière, tout comme l'étage supérieur doté de fenêtres à stores.

LEFT ABOVE:
The entrance gate of rich old teak creates a ligneous portal flanked by tree trunks and mud walls.

LEFT BELOW:
Reflections from the hammered copper washbasin in the upstairs bathroom sparkle like those from the pool framed by a wooden deck.

RIGHT ABOVE:
The architect Cheong Yew Kuang pioneered a rustic approach to ethnic chic in designing an adaptation of a Borneo longhouse for the family of John and Cynthia Hardy.

RIGHT BELOW:
Homemade beeswax candles illuminate the pathway to this two-storied wonder, the lower level of which provides open-air living space among supports made of recycled telegraph poles and tree trunks.

LINKS OBEN:
Die Pforte aus alten Teakholz bildet ein Portal, das von Baumstämmen und Lehmwänden flankiert wird.

LINKS UNTEN:
Das handgehämmerte kupferne Waschbecken im oberen Badezimmer glitzert wie der Pool im unten liegenden Garten.

RECHTE SEITE OBEN:
Architekt Cheong Yew Kuang hat für den Familienbesitz von John und Cynthia Hardy mit seiner Adaption eines Langhauses aus Borneo einen neuen rustikalen „Ethno-Stil" entworfen.

RECHTE SEITE UNTEN:
Hausgemachte Bienenwachskerzen säumen nachts den Pfad, der zu dem zweigeschossigen architektonischen Wunderwerk führt. Die untere Ebene, die aus wiederverwerteten Telegrafenmasten und Baumstämmen konstruiert ist, bildet einen luftigen Wohnbereich.

EN HAUT, À GAUCHE:
Le portail en superbe teck ancien s'inscrit dans des murs de terre flanqués de troncs d'arbre.

EN BAS, À GAUCHE:
Dans la chambre à l'étage, le lave-mains en cuivre martelé brille de mille feux, faisant écho au scintillement de la piscine en contrebas.

PAGE DE DROITE, EN HAUT:
Avec cette adaptation d'une maison allongée de Bornéo pour la propriété familiale de John et Cynthia Hardy, l'architecte Cheong Yew Kuang a introduit le style ethnique rustique chic.

PAGE DE DROITE, EN BAS:
La nuit, des bougies en cire d'abeille de fabrication maison bordent le chemin menant à cette merveille sur deux niveaux. Au rez-de-chaussée, un espace de vie ouvert est délimité par des poteaux télégraphiques et des troncs d'arbres ancrés symétriquement.

CYNTHIA & JOHN HARDY / UBUD

LEFT:
The center pillar and stairway base are made of mud and bamboo, a trademark of combined construction materials used intermittently throughout the compound.

RIGHT ABOVE:
Giant conch shells and an old grinding stone blend into a corner display.

RIGHT BELOW:
The kitchen, surrounded by glass doors and vertical beams, is visible from all sides.

FOLLOWING PAGE LEFT:
Glass doors open up to the dining area where two shell-beaded, ceremonial, children's jackets from Sumatra are displayed on an wall of woven, plastered bamboo.

FOLLOWING PAGE RIGHT:
A comfortable Chinese wedding bed is offered as additional seating in the dining area.

LINKE SEITE:
Der zentrale Pfeiler und das Treppenfundament bestehen aus Lehm und Bambus – ein typisches Beispiel für einen Baumaterialverbund, wie man ihn auf dem gesamten Gelände findet.

RECHTS OBEN:
Riesige Schneckenmuscheln und ein alter Schleifstein zieren eine Ecke.

RECHTS UNTEN:
Die von Glastüren und senkrechten Balken umgebene Küche ist von allen Seiten einsehbar.

FOLGENDE DOPPELSEITE LINKS:
Auf den Wänden aus vergipstem Bambusgeflecht hängen zwei mit Muschelketten verzierte Kinderjäckchen aus Sumatra, die ursprünglich zeremoniellen Zwecken dienten.

FOLGENDE DOPPELSEITE RECHTS:
Ein bequemes chinesisches Hochzeitsbett steht als zusätzliche Sitzgelegenheit im Essbereich zur Verfügung.

PAGE DE GAUCHE:
Le pilier central et le départ de l'escalier sont constitués de terre et de bambou, mariage de matériaux de construction que l'on retrouve çà et là sur la propriété.

EN HAUT, À DROITE:
Arrangement réussi de coquillages démesurés et d'une vieille meule dans un coin.

EN BAS, À DROITE:
La cuisine fermée par des portes vitrées entre des piliers verticaux est visible de tous les côtés.

PAGE SUIVANTE À GAUCHE:
Les deux vestes de cérémonie pour enfants agrémentées de coquillages qui sont accrochées au mur proviennent de Sumatra.

PAGE SUIVANTE À DROITE:
Un confortable lit nuptial chinois constitue un siège supplémentaire dans le coin repas.

CYNTHIA & JOHN HARDY / UBUD

The material used to cover the exposed living area's cushions and pillows is in shades of orange, like those worn by Buddhist monks in Thailand, and blends in with the golden hues of the sunset.

Die Kissen und Polster der offenen Sitzgruppe sind mit Stoffen in Gelb- und Orangetönen bezogen, wie sie die buddhistischen Mönche in Thailand tragen. Die Farben gehen sanft über in die Farbtöne des goldenen Sonnenuntergangs.

Les coussins des sièges en bois sont habillés d'etoffes jaunes et orange, que portent aussi les moines bouddhistes en Thailande. Leurs couleurs fusionnent en douceur avec celles du soleil conchant.

CYNTHIA & JOHN HARDY / UBUD

Mud walls line the periphery of the compound with fertile earthen tones and ferns growing right out of the cracks.

Farne wachsen aus den Rissen der Lehmwände, die das Grundstück nach außen hin in warmen Erdtönen abgrenzen.

La propriété est ceinte par un mur de terre aux tons ocre dans les fissures duquel des fougères ont établi domicile.

102

LEFT ABOVE:
The copper washbasin fitted into a wooden base faces garden palms and Mother Nature's tropical graces.

LEFT BELOW:
From the Kohler bathtub there is a view of rice fields in the valley below and a panorama of the volcanoes in the distance. On clear days even the ocean along the southern coast can be seen.

RIGHT:
A the master bedroom with kilim rugs covering textured wooden floors is adorned with graciously affixed muslin nets and drapes.

LINKS OBEN:
Vom kupfernen Waschbecken, das in eine hölzerne Halterung eingepasst wurde, blickt man auf tropische Gartenpalmen.

LINKS UNTEN:
Von der Kohler-Badewanne aus genießt man den Panoramablick über ein Tal mit Reisfeldern und Vulkanen, und an einem klaren Tag erkennt man sogar das Meer jenseits der südlichen Gestade der Insel.

RECHTE SEITE:
Im Hauptschlafzimmer zieren Kelimteppiche die Holzfußböden und geschmackvoll drapierte Musselinstoffe das Bett und die Fenster.

EN HAUT, À GAUCHE:
Le lave-mains en cuivre encastré dans une console en bois fait face aux palmiers du jardin et aux splendeurs tropicales.

EN BAS, À GAUCHE:
Depuis cette baignoire Kohler, on a vue sur la vallée couverte de rizières, avec en toile de fond les volcans et, par temps clair, sur l'océan au large des côtes sud de l'île.

PAGE DE DROITE:
Les kilims sur les planchers rustiques ainsi que les voilages et moustiquaires en mousseline joliment noués font le charme de cette chambre de maîtres.

104

CYNTHIA & JOHN HARDY / UBUD

AN OLD JAVA HOUSE

CYNTHIA & JOHN HARDY
UBUD

This century-old, one-room, teak residence once owned by a minor Javanese court official caught John and Cynthia Hardy's eyes in the midst of concrete houses in a developing area of central Java where it was being used as a storeroom. They dismantled the house and had it reassemble as a guest house within the Hardy compound. Its walls and beams are hand-hewn, teak and held together by wooden pegs. Decorative traces of the original greenish blue exterior paint contribute to the weathered patina of this lovingly restored home. Its interior features wooden screens, carved interior panels, rustic cushioned chairs and a bed with crisp cotton sheets and flowing white mosquito nets. The small open bathroom they added preserves the mood with its hammered copper sink and a primitive Javanese ladder, used as a towel rack. On the teak deck, smoothed down by generations of bare feet, Cynthia does for her daily yoga exercises while overlooking the young teak trees that shade this precious jewel.

The walls and beams of the old Javanese guest house, once owned by a court official, are hand-hewn slabs of solid teak with traces of the original vintage paint weathered by ten decades of time.

Die Wände und Balken des alten javanischen Gästehauses, das einst einem Justizbeamten gehörte, bestehen aus massiven, handbehauenen Teakholzbrettern, die noch Spuren der ursprünglichen, im Laufe von zehn Jahrzehnten verwitterten Lackierung aufweisen.

Dans cette vieille maison javanaise, qui a appartenu autrefois à un fonctionnaire, les planches et les poutres mises en œuvre ont été taillées à la main dans du teck robuste et portent la trace de la peinture d'origine passée au fil d'un siècle.

Einst gehörte dieses Jahrhunderte alte Teakhaus, das nur aus einem einzigen Raum besteht, einem einfachen Justizbeamten auf Java. Später wurde es inmitten einer Betonsiedlung in Zentraljava als Lagerhalle zweckentfremdet – bis Cynthia und John Hardy das Gebäude entdeckten und erwarben. Sie ließen es abbauen und auf ihrem balinesischen Grundstück als Gästehaus wieder errichten. Die Wände bestehen nach wie vor aus handbearbeiteten Teakholzbalken, die nach alter Tradition nur mit hölzernen Keilen zusammengesteckt werden und vollkommen auf Nägel verzichten. Auch der ehemals grün-blaue Anstrich lässt sich noch erahnen – er verleiht dem liebevoll renovierten Häuschen Charme und Patina. Vor allem Cynthia genießt das historisch-natürliche Ambiente jeden Tag: Sie nutzt das javanische Haus für ihre täglichen Yoga-Übungen und entspannt beim Blick auf die Schatten spendenden Teakbäume.

John et Cynthia Hardy ont eu un coup de cœur pour cette construction en teck centenaire qui appartenait jadis à un petit magistrat javanais. Ce n'était alors qu'un entrepôt abandonné, coincé dans une rangée de maisons en béton dans une zone en développement du centre de Java. Pour créer cette pension, il a fallu démonter la maison, en transporter jusqu'à la propriété des Hardy les murs et les plafonds faits de planches taillées à la main dans des blocs de teck robuste, puis rassembler ces éléments par des chevilles en teck. Des restes de la peinture bleu-vert d'origine, d'une grande qualité décorative, donnent une certaine patine à cette maison restaurée avec amour. Ouverte sur l'extérieur, une petite salle de bains dotée d'un lavabo en cuivre martelé a été subtilement intégrée dans ce cadre par le biais d'une échelle javanaise rustique tenant lieu de porte-serviettes. Sur le pont en teck foulé pendant des années par des pieds nus, Cynthia fait aujourd'hui son yoga quotidien, le regard perdu dans les jeunes tecks qui ombragent la demeure.

LEFT:
The perfectly preserved one-room residence with lavishly carved walls enjoys a dignified retirement.

RIGHT ABOVE:
The rustic, side porch is a private area with a Javanese style chaise lounge for quiet afternoons of reading or gazing at the side garden.

RIGHT BELOW:
A bathroom space, where a primitive ladder serves as a towel rack, is sequestered behind wooden screens.

LINKE SEITE:
Das vollkommen erhaltene Einzimmerwohnhaus mit reich geschnitzten Wänden genießt einen würdevollen Altersruhestand.

RECHTS OBEN:
Die rustikale Seitenveranda bildet einen Privatbereich mit einer Chaiselongue im javanischen Stil für ruhige Nachmittage zum Schmökern oder zum Bewundern des üppigen Gartens.

RECHTS UNTEN:
Vor Blicken aus dem Garten schützen hölzerne Schirmwände den Badbereich, in dem eine urtümliche Leiter als Handtuchhalter dient.

PAGE DE GAUCHE:
Cette maison à pièce unique parfaitement conservée, avec des cloisons richement sculptées, savoure une retraite digne.

EN HAUT, À DROITE:
Ce porche latéral d'une grande simplicité est une zone privée où l'on peut passer des après-midi tranquilles à lire ou contempler le jardin, assis dans une chaise longue de style javanais.

EN BAS, À DROITE:
Ce paravent en bois protège des regards la salle de bains dans laquelle une échelle sommaire tient lieu de porte-serviettes.

AN OLD JAVA HOUSE / UBUD

THE SHRIMP HOUSE

CYNTHIA & JOHN HARDY
UBUD

After descending eighty-two steps down a spiral stair-
case on a steep hillside, crossing a suspension bridge and using
steppingstones to traverse natural springs, one enters a magical world. Nestled in this scenic spot are miniature rice fields,
working fishponds, organic food production, a family of albino
water buffalo and a reassembled antique Javanese house transformed into a thriving shrimp farm. The frame and flooring of
the one-room house is made of teak joists; tempered glass has
been installed to provide a view into a natural pond used to
breed fresh-water shrimp. This unique perspective is most ef-
fective when the water is illuminated to reveal the shrimp. The
farm, with its decoratively cushioned verandah and teak walls
put together without nails, is integrated into this valley setting.
Gigantic lily pads from the Amazon grow in the fishponds, and
trees around the edge provide shade. Local Balinese come to
the river in their everyday activities, evoking scenes of a simpler
life.

The century-old walls
of this teak structure,
now called "The Shrimp
House," are joined
together without nails.

*Die Jahrhunderte alten
Wände dieses Java-Hau-
ses aus Teakholz, das nun
den Namen „The Shrimp
House" trägt, werden
vollkommen ohne Nägel
zusammengehalten.*

*Cette maison en javanaise
teck vieille d'un siècle et
désormais connue sous le
nom de «Shrimp House»,
est assemblée sans clous.*

Wer die 80 Stufen der gewundenen Treppe hinabsteigt, die vor dem Haupthaus der Hardys in den steilen Hang gebaut wurde, über die Hängebrücke geht und auf Trittsteinen eine natürliche Quelle überquert, erreicht eine Bilderbuchlandschaft: mit Reisfeldern im Miniaturformat, einem Fischteich, in dem es vor Leben nur so plätschert, einer Familie von Albino-Wasserbüffeln und einem antiken javanischen Haus, das heute eine Garnelenfarm beherbergt. Den Fußboden des Gebäudes bilden Teakholzbalken, in die gehärtete Glasscheiben eingefügt wurden. Durch sie blickt man direkt auf einen Brutteich mit Süßwassergarnelen – dank der raffinierten Unterwasserbeleuchtung bietet sich hier ein faszinierendes Schauspiel. Am Rand der Fischteiche, auf denen riesige Seerosenblätter aus dem Amazonasgebiet schwimmen, wachsen mächtige Bäume, die das Gelände schützen. Und die einheimischen Balinesen, die hierher zur Arbeit kommen, machen das beschauliche Bild vom schlicht-schönen Landleben perfekt.

Après avoir descendu les 82 marches d'un escalier en colimaçon à flanc de falaise prenant dans la propriété des Hardy, franchi un pont suspendu et traversé un passage à gué dans des sources naturelles, le visiteur découvre un endroit idyllique avec des rizières miniatures, des bassins de pisciculture, des aliments biologiques, une famille de buffles d'Asie et, sur la rivière, une ferme de crevettes prospère, autour d'une maison javanaise ancienne remontée à cet endroit. Le sol de cette maison en teck à pièce unique est constitué de solives dans ce même bois, avec du verre trempé comme élément de remplissage. Un éclairage dans l'eau met en valeur le spectacle unique qu'offre le bassin aux crevettes sous ce plancher vitré. Avec sa véranda agrémentée de coussins et ses murs en teck assemblés sans clous, la maison s'intègre parfaitement dans cette petite vallée. Les bassins à poissons recouverts de gigantesques nénuphars de l'Amazone sont bordés d'arbres qui dispensent de l'ombre aux Balinais vaquant ici à leurs activités quotidiennes.

LEFT ABOVE:
Cynthia Hardy with daughters Carina and Chiara observing koi in a fishpond.

LEFT BELOW:
A silver water pitcher and decorative goblet bordered with the "dot" motif from the Hardy Collection.

RIGHT ABOVE:
Meandering walkways over spring-fed fishponds become a site for family gatherings.

RIGHT BELOW:
"The Shrimp House and its environment honor the landscape while producing food in a natural way," claims Hardy.

LINKS OBEN:
Cynthia Hardy mit ihren Töchtern Carina und Chiara betrachtet einen der Koi-Fischteiche.

LINKS UNTEN:
Ein silberner Wasserkrug und ein dekorativer Becher, deren Ränder mit „Punkt"-Motiven verziert sind, stammen aus der Hardy-Kollektion.

RECHTE SEITE OBEN:
Aus natürlichen Quellen gespeiste Fischteiche mit darüber gelegten Gehwegen werden zu Treffpunkten, an denen sich die Familie versammelt.

RECHTE SEITE UNTEN:
„The Shrimp House", nimmt Rücksicht auf die Landschaft und bringt gleichzeitig auf natürliche Weise Nahrung hervor", erklärt John Hardy.

EN HAUT, À GAUCHE:
Cynthia Hardy observant avec ses filles Carina et Chiara les bassins regorgeant de carpes koi.

EN BAS, À GAUCHE:
cruche et verre à pied en argent ornés du motif «pointillé» de la Collection Hardy.

PAGE DE DROITE, EN HAUT:
Le réseau de ponts de bois enjambant les bassins alimentés par des sources est un point de rencontre pour la famille.

PAGE DE DROITE, EN BAS:
«La Shrimp House et son environnement rendent hommage au paysage tout en produisant de la nourriture de manière naturelle», affirme John Hardy.

THE SHRIMP HOUSE / UBUD

"Flowing water has been the lifeline of Bali's rice-growing tradition for centuries."

„Fließendes Wasser ist seit Jahrhunderten der Lebenssaft für die Reis-bautradition Balis", sagt John Hardy.

«Depuis des siècles, l'eau vive est capitale pour la tradition rizicole balinaise» dit John Hardy.

114

LEFT ABOVE:
Conserving architecture and nature are part of the same sustainable plan.

LEFT BELOW:
Old teak joists frame a floor of tempered glass that exposes a view of the shrimp beneath.

RIGHT:
"Every place on the property is about organic food".

LINKS OBEN:
Sowohl die traditionelle Baukunst als auch die Natur intakt zu erhalten, sind Bestandteile der Philosophie John und Cynthia Hardys.

LINKS UNTEN:
Alte Deckenträger aus Teakholz dienen als Rahmen für die gehärteten Glasscheiben des Fußbodens, durch die man die darunter liegende Garnelenfarm beobachten kann.

RECHTE SEITE:
„Auf diesem Grundstück dreht sich alles um biologische Nahrung."

EN HAUT, À GAUCHE:
La préservation de l'architecture et la protection de la nature s'inscrivent dans le même projet de développement durable.

EN BAS, À GAUCHE:
Du verre trempé comme élément de remplissage entre de vieilles solives en teck dévoile la ferme d'élevage de crevettes.

PAGE DE DROITE :
«Tout, dans cette propriété est en rapport avec la nourriture biologique.»

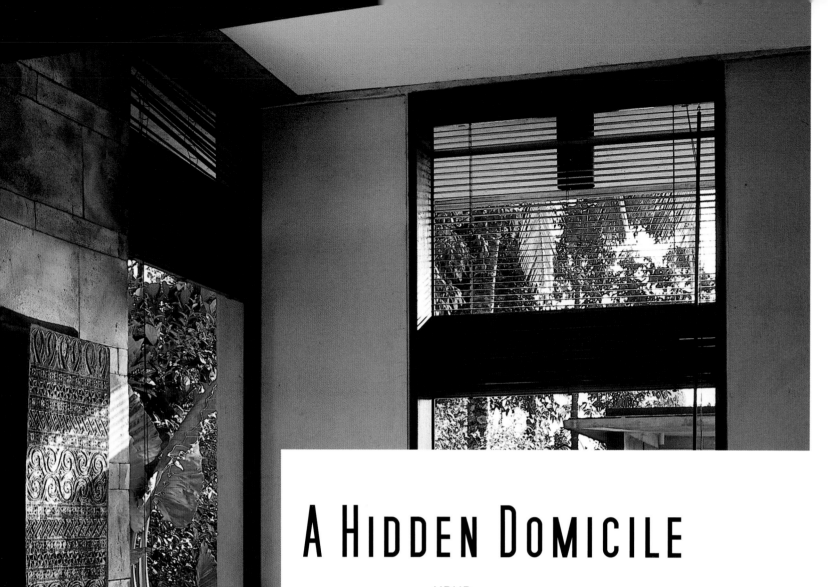

A Hidden Domicile

UBUD

When traveling down the winding roads that lead north from Ubud, to tiny villages located along streams running through wild bamboo forests, one finds people who live more traditional Balinese lives in lush valleys bounded by two mighty rivers. The shop of a family of tile makers from this region marks the hidden driveway to a home guarded by two gorgeous golden retrievers still dripping with water from a morning swim in the 25-meter pool or in one of the many lotus ponds at the entrance to this domicile. The force of its powerful design leads us to a view of a seemingly endless valley on the other side. The earthen tones of the rust colored wall tiles, made by hand next door, define sections of the walkways and sheltered open spaces. The view from the streamlined bathroom's full-length window extends over the pool and merges into the endless vista of the sloping landscape. The innovative design of the modern architecture includes customized furniture made of thick hardwoods. The "U"-shaped layout surrounds a garden of open lawns with scattered frangipani trees.

119

An open window over the tub in the master bathroom overlooks the 25-meter pool; it allows natural light to enter both directly and through reflection.

Von der Badewanne des Hauptschlafzimmers blickt man durch ein offenes Fenster unmittelbar auf ein 25 Meter langes Schwimmbecken. Die Reflexionen auf dem Wasser hellen den Raum mit natürlichem Licht auf.

Une fenêtre ouverte établit une continuité entre la baignoire de la chambre de maîtres et le bassin de 25 mètres de long, multipliant ainsi les reflets de la lumière naturelle dans l'eau.

Von Ubud aus ziehen sich serpentinenreiche Straßen nach Norden – in ein üppig grünes Tal zwischen zwei mächtigen Flüssen, voller Bambushaine und kleiner Dörfer, in denen die Zeit langsamer zu verstreichen scheint als anderswo und die herrliche Aussichten auf eine weitgehend unberührte Natur eröffnen. Die Zufahrt zu diesem versteckten Anwesen ist nicht ganz einfach zu finden – am besten, man hält nach den wunderschönen Golden Retrievern Ausschau, der sie bewacht. Dann kommt man an Lotusteichen vorbei, sieht weit ins Tal hinein und bewundert die innovative Architektur des Hauses, die verschiedenen Erdtöne der Wandfliesen, die gleich nebenan in Handarbeit hergestellt werden, und das maßgefertigte Mobiliar aus robusten Harthölzern. Ein stromlinienförmiges Badezimmer mit überdimensionalem Fenster schließt an den Swimming-Pool an, der am Abhang in die Unendlichkeit zu fließen scheint, und im Garten blüht Roter Jasmin.

Le voyageur qui s'aventure sur les routes en lacet au nord d'Ubud ne rencontre que des villages traditionnels, des torrents, des forêts de bambous et découvre une vallée luxuriante où confluent deux grandes rivières. Une briqueterie familiale marque l'entrée du chemin dérobé aux regards qui mène à une maison gardée par deux superbes golden retrievers, dégoulinant de leur bain matinal dans la piscine de 25 mètres de long ou d'un petit plongeon dans l'un des nombreux bassins à lotus qui bordent l'entrée. La construction audacieuse, qui témoigne d'un parti pris architectural innovant, est tout entière tendue vers une vue imprenable sur la vallée. La large palette de tons ocre des murs en briques fabriquées de manière artisanale à deux pas de là, rythme les coursives sur lesquelles s'ouvrent des espaces ouverts flanqués de chambres. Une salle de bains aux lignes épurées se fond dans l'infini du paysage en contrebas. La maison, qui abrite des meubles en bois durs spécialement conçus, forme un U enserrant des pelouses qu'égaient des frangipaniers.

An angular archway of mud-brick tiles has a concrete roof with a circular opening through the top. Its shade accents the long pool.

RIGHT:
The golden retrievers Mocha and Kara consider the entryway to the house, which spans a lily pond, their territory.

LINKE SEITE:
Ein eckiger Torbogen über dem Pool aus handgefertigten Lehmziegelkacheln und mit einem Betondach, in das eine runde Öffnung eingelassen ist, akzentuiert den langen Pool und spendet Schatten.

RECHTE SEITE:
Die Golden Retriever Mocha und Kara bewachen den Eingangsbereich, der von Seerosenteichen umgeben ist.

PAGE DE GAUCHE:
Une arche anguleuse en briques de terre et dotée d'un toit en béton percé d'une ouverture circulaire dispensant un peu d'ombre rompt la continuité de la longue piscine.

120

PAGE DE DROITE:
Les golden retrievers Mocha et Kara montent la garde à l'entrée agrémentée de bassins où flottent des nénuphars.

124

PREVIOUS DOUBLE PAGE LEFT ABOVE:
The terraced hillside with vegetable gardens plunges into a massive lush gorge where two rivers intersect.

PREVIOUS DOUBLE PAGE LEFT BELOW:
The rectangular archway over the pool connects to another structure, emphasizing its innovative architectural design.

PREVIOUS DOUBLE PAGE RIGHT ABOVE:
A discrete balance of planes of concrete and brick create a home that is more about space and "less about form or "image."

PREVIOUS DOUBLE PAGE RIGHT BELOW:
The wooden deck is literally suspended over stunning views of the forest.

LEFT ABOVE:
A view of the bathroom's vertical window opening from the swimming pool.

LEFT BELOW:
Blooming moon orchids thrive in the cooler climate of the mountains of Bali.

RIGHT ABOVE:
A blazing night fire in a concrete pit on the edge of the open living area.

RIGHT BELOW:
Simple and tasteful bedrooms are functional spaces surrounding the courtyards; they are modeled after the design of traditional Balinese compounds.

VORHERIGE DOPPELSEITE LINKS OBEN:
Der terrassenförmige Hang führt mit seinen Gemüsegärten hinab in eine Schlucht.

VORHERIGE DOPPELSEITE LINKS UNTEN:
Der rechteckige Bogen über dem Pool stellt den Übergang zu einem anderen Gebäude her.

VORHERIGE DOPPELSEITE RECHTS OBEN:
Die verschiedenen Ebenen aus Beton, Holz und Ziegeln zielen darauf, dass Raum eine größere Rolle als Form oder „Aussehen" spielt.

VORHERIGE DOPPELSEITE RECHTS UNTEN:
Die Terrasse aus Holzplanken mit atemberaubendem Panorama hängt buchstäblich über dem Wald.

LINKS OBEN:
Ein Blick aus dem Badezimmerfenster auf das Schwimmbecken.

LINKS UNTEN:
Blühende Nachtfalterorchideen (Malayenblumen) gedeihen prächtig im kühleren Bergklima Balis.

RECHTE SEITE OBEN:
Ein loderndes Nachtfeuer in einer Feuerstelle aus Beton am Rande des offenen Wohnbereichs.

RECHTE SEITE UNTEN:
Schlichte und geschmackvolle Schlafzimmer befinden sich in den Randbereichen um Innenhöfe, was auf traditionelle balinesische Grundrisse zurückgeht.

DOUBLE PAGE PRÉCÉDENTE, EN HAUT À GAUCHE:
Le jardin potager en terrasses plonge dans la gorge luxuriante où confluent deux rivières.

DOUBLE PAGE PRÉCÉDENTE, EN BAS À GAUCHE:
L'arche anguleuse qui enjambe la piscine est reliée à une autre structure, mettant en valeur le caractère novateur de son architecture.

DOUBLE PAGE PRÉCÉDENTE, EN HAUT À DROITE:
Un équilibre discret entre des surfaces de béton et de briques tend à créer une maison davantage axée sur l'espace que sur la forme ou le «look».

DOUBLE PAGE PRÉCÉDENTE, EN BAS À DROITE:
Cette terrasse en caillebotis est littéralement suspendue au-dessus des forêts saisissantes de beauté.

EN HAUT, À GAUCHE:
la fenêtre ouverte de la salle de bains vue depuis la piscine.

EN BAS, À GAUCHE:
Les orchidées, ici une phalaenopsis amabilis, prospèrent dans le climat relativement frais des montagnes de Bali.

PAGE DE DROITE, EN HAUT:
Un feu crépitant dans le foyer en béton en bordure de l'espace salon ouvert.

PAGE DE DROITE, EN BAS:
Des chambres simples, mais aménagées avec goût, sont disposées autour de cours, évoquant l'architecture des propriétés traditionnelles de Bali.

LEFT ABOVE:
The bathroom´s modern flair exudes warmth with natural wood finishing and ligneous patterned accents.

LEFT BELOW:
The bedroom's serene ambience is underlined by light and shadows.

RIGHT:
The sun-dried mud-brick tiles in earthen tones, made in the compound next door, are a dominant background theme, lining courtyards, ponds and passageways in this home.

LINKS OBEN:
Der Gebrauch von verschiedenen Hölzern gibt dem modernen Flair des Badezimmers Wärme.

LINKS UNTEN:
Das Schlafzimmer bietet mit seinen Licht- und Schattenspielen ein Ambiente der Heiterkeit und der Gelassenheit.

RECHTE SEITE:
Die sonnengetrockneten Lehmziegelkacheln in Erdtönen, die auf dem Nachbargrundstück hergestellt werden, bilden in diesem Haus die Hintergründe entlang der Höfe, Teiche und Korridore.

EN HAUT, À GAUCHE:
Le style moderne des salles de bain doit sa chaleur aux finitions en bois naturel et aux veinures du bois.

EN BAS, À GAUCHE:
Dans la chambre, des lignes d'ombres et de lumière créent une ambiance sereine et décontractée.

PAGE DE DROITE:
Les briques de terre séchées au soleil, fabriquées sur la propriété voisine, sont une caractéristique dominante de cette maison, dont elles parent cours, bassins et couloirs de tons ocre.

126

A HIDDEN DOMICILE / UBUD

Rabik Estate

AMIR RABIK
UBUD

During his school days on the island of Madura, northwest of Bali, Amir Rabik began collecting traditional Indonesian art. Now involved with telecommunications, and Spain's honorary consul in Bali, Amir Rabik is really an ambassador to the eccentric elite who visit the island and find his creative outlook, humor and hospitality charismatic. The Rabik Estate in Ubud beckons spirits of the past with its vast collection of primitive works of religious art found throughout his exhibit space and extensive home, which is perched high up on a hill overlooking a river gorge and coconut trees beyond. A rising full moon casts lunar shadows on terraces and towering trees, all planted by Amir. He has also always been his own architect, responsible for the construction and design of this compound, which he began to build in 1980. Coconut, thick natural wood and mother-of-pearl inlay are characteristic of his prolific work as a furniture designer. Both his talent and his eye for the essential are impressive.

A twenty-five-year-old banyan tree, planted when Amir Rabik's second son Karim was born, now has a towering trunk. With its numerous offshoots and branching limbs it has become a holy tree.

Ein Affenbrotbaum, der vor über 25 Jahren, zur Zeit der Geburt des ersten Sohnes, Karim, gepflanzt wurde, ist heute mit seinem prächtigen Stamm und seinen weit ausladenden Ästen und Zweigen ein „heiliger" Baum.

Un banian planté à la naissance de leur premier fils, Karim, il y a plus de 25 ans, est maintenant un arbre sacré avec son tronc principal s'élançant vers le ciel d'où partent de grosses branches et des troncs secondaires.

Amir Rabik ist ein Liebhaber traditioneller indonesischer Kunst, spanischer Honorarkonsul auf Bali und Botschafter jener exzentrischen Elite, die regelmäßig auf die Insel reist und sich in ihren Bann ziehen lässt. Wer Sinn für Kreativität, Humor und Lebensfreude hat, wohnt bei solchen Besuchen auf Rabik Estate, wo Kunstobjekte der Naturvölker die Geister der Vergangenheit beschwören und eine schier endlose Zahl von Ausstellungsräumen sowie die Privatgemächer des Hausherren füllen. Die persönlichen Wohnräume liegen hoch oben auf einem Berg und blicken über eine Felsschlucht, durch die ein Fluss rauscht, sowie auf Kokospalmen, die sich sanft in Wind wiegen. Amir Rabik begann 1980 mit dem Bau und zeichnet höchstpersönlich für alle architektonischen und gestalterischen Aspekte verantwortlich. Dass er als Designer Talent hat, zeigen besonders die Möbel aus Kokospalmenholz und anderen robusten Naturhölzern, die er mit schimmernden Perlmuttintarsien wirkungsvoll verziert hat.

Amir Rabik collectionne l'art traditionnel indonésien depuis son enfance. Travaillant dans le secteur des télécommunications et consul honoraire d'Espagne à Bali, il est un ambassadeur pour l'élite excentrique qui visite l'île et apprécie sa créativité, son humour et son hospitalité. La propriété de Rabik à Ubud évoque le passé avec des œuvres d'art primitives d'inspiration religieuse disséminées dans les pièces de son show-room et domicile juché au sommet d'une colline qui domine la gorge creusée par la rivière et, un peu plus loin, les cocoteraies. La pleine lune projette des ombres spectrales sur les terrasses et les arbres imposants, qu'il a tous plantés. En tant qu'architecte, Amir Rabik a eu la maîtrise exclusive de la construction du bâtiment et de l'aménagement de sa propriété qu'il a entrepris doucement dans les années 1980. Dans ses très nombreuses lignes de mobilier, il a accordé une place de choix au bois de coco et à d'autres essences denses incrustées de nacre. Son talent est aussi illimité que son flair pour l'essence adéquate.

LEFT:
A rare phantasmal frog
camouflages a carved
soap-stone escarpment
depicting Wishnu, the god
of gardens and prosperity.

RIGHT:
A view of the structure
harboring the art gallery
can be seen from the
stony walkway that serves
as an entrance to the
estate.

LINKE SEITE:
Ein seltener Frosch
sitzt getarnt auf einer in
Seifenstein gehauenen
Gottheit, Wischnu, einem
Schutzgott der Gärten und
des Wohlstands.

RECHTE SEITE:
Wenn man den steinernen
Gehweg am Eingang zum
Grundstück hinabgeht,
sieht man das Gebäude,
in dem die Kunstgalerie
untergebracht ist.

PAGE DE GAUCHE :
Une grenouille fantoma-
tique se camoufle dans
une sculpture de stéatite
représentant Vishnu, le
dieu de l'abondance et de
la prospérité.

130   PAGE DE DROITE:
En empruntant le chemin
de pierre qui mène à la
propriété, on découvre la
construction abritant la
galerie d'art.

PREVIOUS DOUBLE PAGE LEFT:
A thatched wooden lantern among green river rocks leads the way to a three-tiered wanitlan structure, reminiscent of Bali's royal temple sites.

PREVIOUS DOUBLE PAGE RIGHT:
Nepalese architecture also inspired Rabik to build this guest house with a meditation tower on top.

LEFT ABOVE:
An altar of Buddha statues enshrine the painting of the supreme Balinese god, Ida San Hyang Widi Wasa, by master Ubud artist, Ketut Budiana.

LEFT BELOW:
A bronze statue of Amitaba represents the transitional era of Hinduism to Buddhism in Java.

RIGHT:
Old terracotta and Chinese celadon pots are scattered throughout the plenteous garden.

FOLLOWING DOUBLE PAGE LEFT:
A magical mist from the compound's valley-view dining patio unveils the majesty of the tropical forests, paying homage to the gods with a shrine.

FOLLOWING DOUBLE PAGE RIGHT:
The sinuous roots of the banyan tree intertwine, forming a natural sculpture and providing food for contemplation while sitting in the restful sitting pavilion nearby.

VORIGE DOPPELSEITE LINKS:
Eine mit Stroh gedeckte Holzlaterne weist den Weg zu einem dreistöckigen wanitlan-Bau, der an die Königstempel Balis erinnert.

VORIGE DOPPELSEITE RECHTS:
Die nepalesische Baukunst inspirierte Rabik auch, dieses Gästehaus mit einem Meditationsturm im obersten Stock zu bauen.

LINKS OBEN:
Ein Altar mit Buddhastatuen dient als Schrein für ein Gemälde. Es wurde von Ketut Budiana, einem Meister unter den Künstlern Ubuds, geschaffen.

LINKS UNTEN:
Eine Bronzestatue Amitabas verkörpert die Übergangszeit vom Hinduismus zum Buddhismus auf Java.

RECHTE SEITE:
Alte Terrakottatöpfe und chinesische Celadongefäße sind über den gesamten fruchtbaren Garten verteilt.

FOLGENDE DOPPELSEITE LINKS:
Vor der Essveranda mit Talblick enthüllt ein magischer Nebel die majestätische Pracht des Tropenwaldes. Den Göttern zollt man mit einem Schrein Tribut.

FOLGENDE DOPPELSEITE RECHTS:
Die verschlungenen Wurzeln des Affenbrotbaums verflechten sich zu einer natürlichen Skulptur und zu Stufen zu einem gemütlichen Sitzpavilion.

PAGE PRÉCÉDENTE, À GAUCHE:
Une lanterne coiffée de chaume parmi les galets verts provenant de la rivière éclaire le chemin menant à un wanitlan, construction sur trois niveaux, qui rappelle les temples royaux de Bali.

PAGE PRÉCÉDENTE, À DROITE:
Rabik a puisé aux sources de l'architecture népalaise l'inspiration pour la construction de ce pavillon pour les invités coiffé d'une tour de méditation.

EN HAUT, À GAUCHE:
Un autel orné de statues de Bouddha confère un caractère sacré à cette peinture représentant le dieu suprême balinais, Ida San Hyang Widi Wasa, œuvre de Ketut Budiana, artiste majeur d'Ubud,

EN BAS, À GAUCHE:
Statue en bronze d'Amitaba représentative de la période de transition entre hindouisme et bouddhisme à Java

PAGE DE DROITE:
Des récipients en terre cuite et des céladons chinois anciens émaillent le jardin luxuriant.

PAGE SUIVANTE À GAUCHE:
Une brume magique s'élevant de la vallée en contrebas dévoile la beauté des forêts tropicales un autel rend hommage aux dieux.

PAGE SUIVANTE À DROITE:
Assis dans ce paisible pavillon, on se plonge dans la contemplation de la sculpture naturelle créée par les racines entrelacées de ce banian.

The three-dimensionally carved old Chinese bed in the guest house is surrounded by coconut wood beams and a wooden chair designed by Rabik.

FOLLOWING DOUBLE PAGE:
A display of part of Rabik's extensive art collection ranging from an exquisite mask from Mali to Moa carvings from the Maluku Islands.

Ein von Rabik entworfener Holzstuhl steht neben dem plastisch geschnitzten, alten chinesischen Bett im Gästehaus.

FOLGENDE DOPPELSEITE:
Hier wird Rabiks Kunstsammlung mit zahlreichen Werken ausgestellt, die von einer „außerirdischen" Maske aus Mali bis zu Moa-Schnitzereien von den Molukken reichen.

Dans le pavillon destiné aux invités, un lit chinois ancien sculpté se marie avec des poutres en bois de coco et avec une chaise en bois signée Rabik.

DOUBLE PAGE SUIVANTE:
138 Dans la salle d'exposition, la collection d'art de Rabik couvre une large palette allant d'un masque «extra-terrestre» sculptés provenant du Mali à des sculptures Moa des îles Moluques.

Uma Ubud

UBUD

The Uma ("living house") resort offers an escape based on holistic physical and mental equilibrium. Hidden away on a 3-hectare site near Ubud, Bali's cultural hub, this ecological sanctuary has tranquil jungles and breathtaking views of the Oos River. The rich textures of the natural landscape were embellished by Trevor Hillier's garden plan. The Japanese interior designer Koichiro Ikebuchi took a puristic approach, using indigenous materials. The effect is a light, flowing simplicity in the white bedrooms decorated with curtains of local cutwork lace and whitewashed furniture. These contrast starkly with the black terrazzo bathrooms. Their shuttered windows line the stone walkways over ponds full of lily pads. The open-air yoga pavilion is used by internationally renowned yoga teachers. Retreats are offered along with guided nature walks, cultural activities and Ayurvedic spa treatments. The Uma experience conveys a sense of balance and holistic awareness, a haven for body and soul.

Light floods the open bath from shiny water fixtures in this sanctuary of indulgence at the Uma Ubud, where privacy promises complete pleasure.

Lichtdurchflutet ist das offene Bad in diesem Allerheiligsten des Verwöhnens bei Uma Ubud, wo der Genuss schon deshalb perfekt ist, weil man vollkommen ungestört ist.

La lumière tombe à flots sur la robinetterie étincelante dans ce sanctuaire du bien-être qu'est Uma Ubud, où la discrétion promet un plaisir complet.

Uma bedeutet übersetzt „lebendes Haus" und ist ein Zufluchtsort für alle, die dem Alltag für einige Zeit entfliehen und die Natur und sich selbst wiederfinden möchten. Die Anlage erstreckt sich über ein drei Hektar großes Gelände am Rande von Ubud, dem kulturellen Zentrum der Insel. Hier lebt man inmitten des Urwaldes und genießt atemberaubende Aussichten auf die Schlucht des Flusses Oos. Der Landschaftsarchitekt Trevor Hillier setzt diese Naturschönheiten wie selbstverständlich in Uma Ubud fort, und auch der Innenarchitekt Koichiro Ikebuchi findet in der Landschaft Inspiration: Er lässt die Räume puristisch wirken und vermittelt mit einheimischen Materialien Leichtigkeit und Schlichtheit. So sind die Schlafzimmer mit weißen Wänden, weißen Möbeln und Spitzenvorhängen ausgestattet und bilden einen wirkungsvollen Kontrast zu den schwarzen Terrazzo-Bädern. Ein traumhafter Platz ist auch der Freiluft-Yoga-Pavillon, in dem international bekannte Lehrer Workshops abhalten – denn in Uma Ubud sollen Körper und Seele ins Gleichgewicht finden.

Uma, la «maison vivante», est un endroit propre aux escapades et à l'aventure empreint d'une philosophie holistique de l'équilibre physique et mental. Ce sanctuaire respectueux de l'environnement est implanté sur une propriété de trois hectares à la lisière de la capitale culturelle de Bali, Ubud, sous le signe d'une forêt vierge paisible et des paysages saisissants des gorges de l'Oos. La nature environnante est encore embellie par le jardin de l'architecte paysager Trevor Hillier. L'architecte d'intérieur japonais Koichiro Ikebuchi a opté pour une esthétique minimaliste mettant en œuvre des matériaux locaux. Il émane une simplicité légère de chaque structure, dotée de chambres aux murs blancs, de rideaux de dentelle traditionnels de la région et de meubles chaulés qui créent un contraste marqué avec les salles de bains en terrazzo noir. A l'étage, le pavillon de yoga ouvert accueille des professeurs de renommée internationale qui animent des retraites. Uma est un havre de paix pour le corps et l'esprit.

144

LEFT ABOVE:
The well-balanced land-scaping reveals an army of carved totem pole adding a primitive awe to the garden scenario.

LEFT BELOW:
Breakfast is served on the Garden Room's patio over-looking an Edenic view of the staggering Oos river gorge with wildlife echoing through unspoilt countryside.

RIGHT ABOVE:
Whether under the roof or under the shade of umbrellas, the "Kemiri" restaurant is simple, yet stylish. Intimate dining can be enjoyed on the edge of a pond fed by a waterfall.

RIGHT BELOW:
The 25-meter swimming pool leads to the two sto-ried main pavilion of the Uma, or 'living house'.

LINKS OBEN:
Die ausgewogene Land-schaftsgestaltung legt eine Armee geschnitzter Totempfähle frei, die dem Gartenszenario eine ur-tümliche Majestät verleiht.

LINKS UNTEN:
Das Frühstück wird auf der Terrasse des „Garden Room" serviert, von der man einen paradiesischen Ausblick auf die schwin-delerregende Schlucht des Flusses Oos genießt und den Lauten wilder Tiere lauschen kann.

RECHTE SEITE OBEN:
Das „Kemiri"-Restaurant ist sowohl in den über-dachten als auch unüber-dachten Bereichen eine schlichte, stilvolle Umge-bung zum Essen neben ei-nem aus einem Wasserfall gespeisten Teich.

RECHTE SEITE UNTEN:
Das 25-Meter-Becken des Swimming-Pools führt auf den zweigeschossi-gen Hauptpavillon des Uma Ubud zu, was so viel wie „lebendiges Haus" bedeutet.

EN HAUT, À GAUCHE:
L'aménagement paysager met en scène une armée de totems sculptés ins-pirant une peur primitive mêlée de respect.

EN BAS, À GAUCHE:
Le petit-déjeuner est servi dans le patio de la Garden Room d'où l'on embrasse du regard les saisissantes gorges de l'Oos. On pent ecouter les animaux sauvages se répondre d'un bout à l'autre de cette région préservée.

PAGE DE DROITE, EN HAUT:
Le restaurant Kemiri, avec une partie couverte et une terrasse, est un îlot simple mais élégant à proximité d'un bassin alimenté par une cascade.

PAGE DE DROITE, EN BAS:
A la tête du bassin de 25 mètres se trouve le pavillon principal sur deux niveaux de l'Uma, «mai-son de vie».

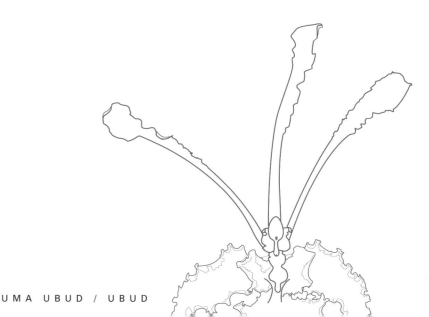

UMA UBUD / UBUD

LEFT:
The Uma's regular yoga instructress demonstrates an extended triangle asana pose during an afternoon yoga class in the upstairs studio, overlooking a tropical garden.

RIGHT:
A canopied walkway with frangipani trees, towering heliconias and flowering shrubs that accent the clean modern angles of the colonnaded stairway of the main pavilion.

LINKE SEITE:
Umas reguläre Yogalehrerin führt in einer nachmittäglichen Yogastunde, die im oben gelegenen Studio mit Blick auf den Tropengarten stattfindet, eine Trikonasana-Stellung (Dreiecksstellung) vor.

RECHTE SEITE:
Ein überdachter Gehweg mit Roten Jasminbäumen, riesigen Helikonien und sich windenden Sträuchern akzentuiert die klaren modernen Winkel des mit Kolonnaden gesäumten Treppenaufgangs am Hauptpavillon.

146 **PAGE DE GAUCHE:**
Le professeur de yoga attitré de l'Uma montrant un triangle (triconasana) dans le cadre d'un cours d'après-midi dans la salle surplombant le jardin tropical.

PAGE DE DROITE:
Un tunnel de verdure constitué par des frangipaniers, et des balisiers géants et des arbustes en fleurs ondoyants met en valeur les angles nets modernes de l'escalier flanqué de colonnes du pavillon principal.

PREVIOUS DOUBLE PAGE LEFT:
This composition created by the landscape architect Trevor Hillier, making use of the indigenous horticultural opulence, is a prime example of the beautiful design of the hotel's gardens.

PREVIOUS DOUBLE PAGE RIGHT:
The lattice work of the woven screens separating the bedroom and outer garden allows a myriad of shadowed patterns to dance in the filtered light of the afternoon sun.

LEFT ABOVE:
The Uma rooms are a haven of space and freshness with muslin-soft cottons and light, flowing, aesthetic interiors by Japanese designer, Koichiro Ikebuchi.

LEFT BELOW:
A private courtyard of water ponds and a garden terrace separate the bedroom from the louvered doors that open to a breathtaking bathroom of black with white highlights.

RIGHT:
The simplicity of the black terrazzo bathroom is the Uma's ultimate sanctuary for a Zen experience of physical relaxation and mental quietude.

VORIGE DOPPELSEITE LINKS:
Diese opulente Komposition aus einheimischen Pflanzen von dem Landschaftsgestalter Trevor Hillier ist ein perfektioniertes Beispiel der für das Hotel entworfenen Gartenpracht.

VORIGE DOPPELSEITE RECHTS:
Das Flechtwerk der Wandschirme, die das Schlafzimmer vom äußeren Garten trennen, wirft eine Unzahl von Schattenmustern.

LINKS OBEN:
Die Uma-Zimmer wirken geräumig und frisch nach Entwürfen des japanischen Designers Koichiro Ikebuchi.

LINKS UNTEN:
Ein Privathof mit Teichen und eine Gartenterrasse trennen das Schlafgemach mit Lamellentüren, das sich zu einem atemberaubenden Badezimmer hin öffnet, in dem Schwarz und Weiß die Akzente setzen.

RECHTE SEITE:
Die Schlichtheit des schwarzen Badezimmers aus Terrazzo bildet den allerletzten Zufluchtsort des Uma für ein Zen-Erlebnis der körperlichen Entspannung und des geistigen Friedens.

PAGE PRÉCÉDENTE, À GAUCHE:
La composition exubérante de végétaux endémiques, œuvre du paysagiste Trevor Hillier, est une parfaite illustration de la splendeur de ce jardin conçu pour un hôtel.

PAGE PRÉCÉDENTE, À DROITE:
Le treillis des paravents tressés qui séparent la chambre du jardin est animé par une myriade d'ombres dansant dans la lumière tamisée du soleil de l'après-midi.

EN HAUT, À GAUCHE:
Les chambres de l'Uma sont un havre d'espace et de fraîcheur avec leurs fines mousselines de coton et leurs aménagements à l'esthétique légère conçus par le styliste japonais Koichiro Ikebuchi.

EN BAS, À GAUCHE:
Une cour privée dotée de bassins et une terrasse-jardin séparent la chambre de la porte à claire-voie qui ouvre sur une salle de bains saisissante en noir et blanc.

PAGE DE DROITE:
Cette salle de bains en terrazzo noir d'une grande simplicité est le sanctuaire suprême de la relaxation physique et de la paix de l'esprit à l'Uma.

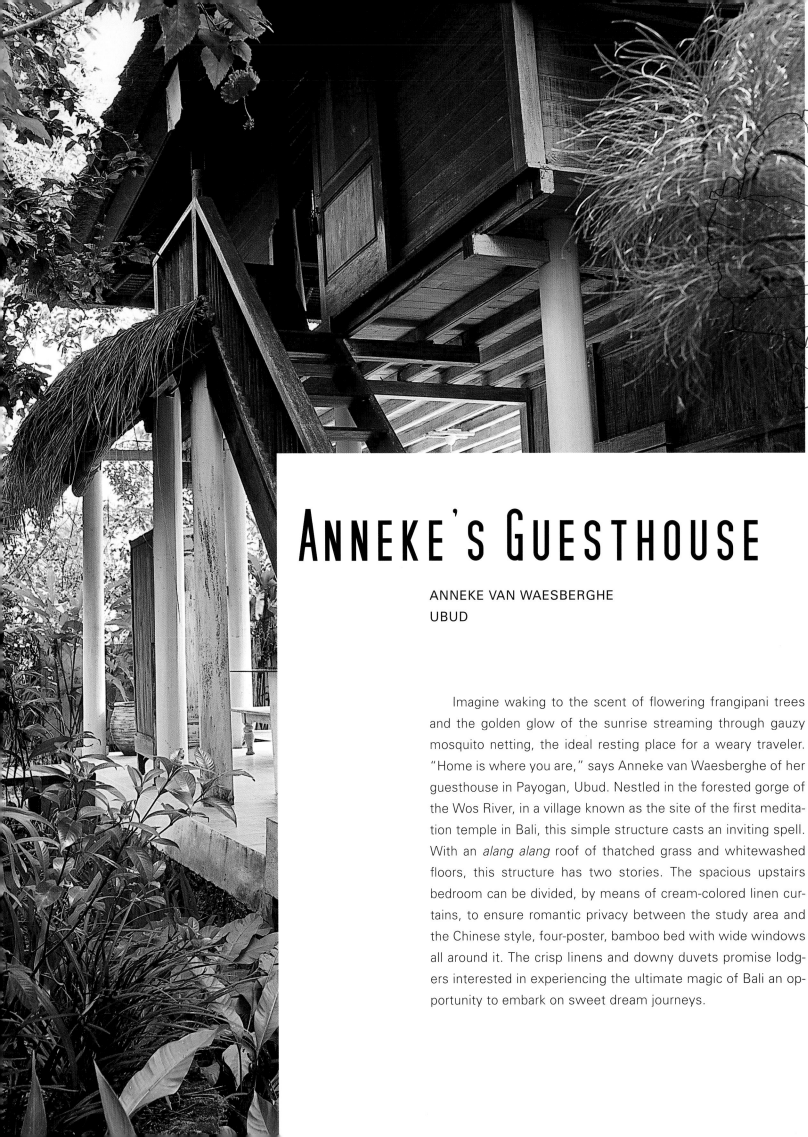

ANNEKE'S GUESTHOUSE

ANNEKE VAN WAESBERGHE
UBUD

Imagine waking to the scent of flowering frangipani trees and the golden glow of the sunrise streaming through gauzy mosquito netting, the ideal resting place for a weary traveler. "Home is where you are," says Anneke van Waesberghe of her guesthouse in Payogan, Ubud. Nestled in the forested gorge of the Wos River, in a village known as the site of the first meditation temple in Bali, this simple structure casts an inviting spell. With an *alang alang* roof of thatched grass and whitewashed floors, this structure has two stories. The spacious upstairs bedroom can be divided, by means of cream-colored linen curtains, to ensure romantic privacy between the study area and the Chinese style, four-poster, bamboo bed with wide windows all around it. The crisp linens and downy duvets promise lodgers interested in experiencing the ultimate magic of Bali an opportunity to embark on sweet dream journeys.

The alang-alang *thatched roof shelters the entrance to the two-storied guesthouse.*

Ein Vordach des zweigeschossigen Gästehauses aus alang-alang *schützt den Eingang zu seinem einladenden Wohnzimmer.*

Un avant-toit en chaume d'alang alang abrite l'entrée de la pension.

153

Es ist der Beginn eines perfekten Tages: Der Duft von blühendem Rotem Jasmin schwebt in der Luft, das goldene Glitzern der aufgehenden Sonne schimmert durch den Schleier des Moskitonetzes, und draußen singen die Vögel um die Wette. Anneke van Waesberghe verwöhnt ihre Gäste mit viel Liebe zum Detail, denn sie ist überzeugt: „Da, wo man sich aufhält, ist man zu Hause!". Ihr Besitz liegt in einer bewaldeten Schlucht des Flusses Wos – in einem Dorf, das den ersten Meditationstempel Balis besaß. Das schlichte zweistöckige Guesthouse mit einem Reetdach aus *alang alang* fasziniert mit einer offenen Bauweise – überall zeichnet das einfallende Licht zarte Muster auf gekälkte Holzböden und hölzerne Wände. Das romantische Bambus-Himmelbett lässt sich durch Leinenvorhänge vom Arbeitsbereich abtrennen und ist mit frisch duftenden Laken bezogen – süße Träume und der Zauber Balis in unverfälschter Form sind hier garantiert.

Imaginez que vous vous réveillez dans un gîte offert au voyageur las, avec le parfum des frangipaniers en fleur dans les narines et l'éclat doré du soleil matinal filtrant à travers la gaze d'une moustiquaire. «On est chez soi, là où l'on est», dit Anneke Van Waesberghe de sa pension à Pagoyan, près d'Ubud. Nichée dans la gorge boisée de la rivière Wos, dans un village qui abrite le premier temple de méditation de Bali connu de temps historiques, cette construction simple à deux étages coiffée d'un toit en *alang alang* est si ouverte qu'elle invite la lumière naturelle à jeter des ombres enchanteresses sur les sols blanchis à la chaux et sur les murs en bois. Dans la vaste chambre entourée de fenêtres ouvertes qui se trouve à l'étage, l'intimité est préservée de manière romantique par des rideaux de lin écru que l'on peut tirer entre le coin bureau et le lit à baldaquin en bambou de style chinois. Les draps bruissants et l'édredon douillet promettent des voyages oniriques nocturnes à tout hôte désireux de sentir la magie profonde de Bali.

LEFT ABOVE:
An antique Javanese desk of solid teak provides a study area in the bedroom with windows on all sides.

LEFT BELOW:
A Balinese terracotta pot filled with fragrant tuberoses, called "sedap malam," decorates an open corner.

RIGHT:
The upstairs bedroom can be divided by a romantic curtain. Mosquito netting of voile is suspended from the four-poster bed. At the foot of the bed is a leather suitcase and traveling bag from another era.

LINKS OBEN:
Ein antiker javanischer Schreibtisch aus massivem Teakholz steht im Schlafbereich im oberen Stockwerk, der rundum von offenen Fenstern umgeben ist.

LINKS UNTEN:
Ein balinesisches Terrakottagefäß, gefüllt mit duftenden Tuberosen namens sedap malam, ziert eine offene Ecke.

RECHTE SEITE:
Den Schlafbereich im oberen Stockwerk teilt ein romantischer Vorhang vom Arbeitsbereich ab. Der Lederkoffer und die Reisetasche wecken Erinnerungen an eine vergangene Epoche.

EN HAUT, À GAUCHE:
A l'étage, un bureau javanais en teck massif marque la limite entre la partie couchage et le coin bureau doté de fenêtres sur tous les côtés.

EN BAS, À GAUCHE:
Un vase en terre cuite rempli de tubéreuses parfumées, qu'on appelle ici sedap malam, orne un angle ouvert.

PAGE DE DROITE:
bagages en cuir d'une autre époque dans l'espace couchage d'un grand romantisme avec son rideau de séparation en mousseline et sa moustiquaire aérienne flottant sur le lit à baldaquin en bambou.

ANNEKE'S GUESTHOUSE / UBUD

ANNEKE VAN WAESBERGHE

UBUD

Dutch-born Anneke van Waesberghe spent years traveling all over the world without any place to call "home." Her employer was based in New York City and had her bringing architects from the East and the West together. This drew her more toward Asia. First she settled in Vietnam, but then fate opened the door for her to explore Bali. She immediately relocated; that was nearly a decade ago. It was a natural progression for Anneke to go on to create her own line of luxurious traveler's accessories called "Esprite Nomade." Its elegant spiral logo, enshrined at the entrance to her home, seems to convey its meaning: that "life is a process." It is the point at which real and virtual travelers meet up with salon adventurers, an impression conveyed by Anneke's neo-colonial home on the banks of a river in Ubud. The weather-worn patina of the furniture, with white and neutral textures, is shrouded by netting and pillows, thereby conjuring the splendor of the past in its many cozy corners.

*Pillows from Vietnam with
hand-painted Chinese
calligraphy create a se-
rene setting. The Art Deco
teapot reminds Anneke of
her grandmother.*

*Kissen aus Vietnam mit
handgemalten Schriftzei-
chen, eine Art Déco-Tee-
kanne, die Anneke an ihre
Oma erinnert, schaffen
eine gemütliche Atmo-
sphäre.*

*Des oreillers provenant
du Viêtnam agrémentés
d'une calligraphie chinoise
peinte à la main s'allient
à une théière Art Déco
qui rappelle à Anneke sa
grand-mère, pour créer
une ambiance d'une gran-
de sérénité.*

Die gebürtige Niederländerin Anneke van Waesberghe reis-
te jahrelang rastlos um den Erdball, ohne dabei ihr wahres Zuhause zu finden. Ihre Firma mit Sitz in New York stellte Kontakte
her zwischen Designern und Architekten aus West und Ost,
und so landete sie in Asien. Aber kaum hatte sie sich in Vietnam niedergelassen und begonnen, dort zu arbeiten, da öffnete
ihr das Schicksal eine andere Tür: Sie lernte Bali kennen und
erkor die Insel vor fast einem Jahrzehnt augenblicklich zu ihrer
neuen Wahlheimat. Das elegante Spiralemblem, das auch am
Eingang ihres Hauses eingelassen ist, versinnbildlicht ihr Mot-
to: „Das Leben ist ein Prozess." Hier treffen Reiselust und vir-
tueller Urlauber auf die Geisteshaltung des Salon-Abenteurers,
wie sie sich auch in Annekes neokolonialistischem Eigenheim
am Flussufer in Ubud spiegelt. Die verwitterte Patina des Mobiliars mit seinen weißen und neutralen Oberflächen, bedeckt
mit Naturfasern und weichen Kissen, weckt Erinnerungen an
den Glanz vergangener Zeiten.

La Hollandaise Anneke van Waesberghe a longtemps par-
couru le monde sans avoir vraiment de chez-soi. Elle a enten-
du l'appel de l'Asie alors qu'elle travaillait pour une organisation
basée à New York et chargée de favoriser les rencontres entre
des stylistes et des architectes occidentaux et orientaux. Elle
pensait avoir trouvé au Viêtnam un endroit où vivre et exercer
sa profession de styliste quand le destin lui a ouvert une nouvelle porte, celle de Bali, où elle s'est aussitôt installée, il y a
bientôt dix ans. « Esprite Nomade », une ligne haut de gamme
d'accessoires pour le voyage, a vu alors tout naturellement le
jour. L'élégant logo en volute à l'entrée illustre sa devise selon
laquelle « la vie est un processus ». Le voyageur, authentique
ou virtuel, et l'aventurier de salon se côtoient ici, dans cette
demeure néocoloniale en bord de rivière, à Ubud. La patine du
mobilier avec ses textures blanches ou neutres, les voilages,
les coussins moelleux et autres accessoires confortables tra-
duisent la splendeur du passé.

LEFT ABOVE:
Anneke models her travel pajamas flanked by decorative twisted trunks from forest vine trees.

LEFT BELOW:
The alfresco shower is an extension of the bathroom, both are constructed of white concrete.

RIGHT:
The simplicity of the cushioned floor with a low Japanese style dining area is enhanced with a painting by Balinese artist, Jiwatson.

LINKS OBEN:
Anneke führt den von ihr selbst entworfenen Reiseschlafanzug vor.

LINKS UNTEN:
Die Dusche im Freien aus Weißbeton bildet eine Verlängerung des Badezimmers aus dem gleichen Material.

RECHTE SEITE:
Die Schlichtheit des Raums mit dem Essbereich im japanischen Stil auf dem Boden wird durch ein Gemälde des balinesischen Künstlers Jiwatson unterstrichen.

EN HAUT, À GAUCHE:
Anneke arbore son pyjama de voyage entre des troncs de lianes noueux.

EN BAS, À GAUCHE:
Béton blanc pour la douche en plein air et la salle de bains dans le prolongement de laquelle elle se situe.

PAGE DE DROITE:
La sobriété des sièges de l'espace repas de style japonais, avec des coussins à même le sol, est mise en valeur par une peinture de l'artiste balinais Jiwatson.

ANNEKE VAN WAESBERGHE / UBUD

The elegant spiral logo of "Esprite Nomade" is enshrined at the entrance, it symbolizes "life as a process."

RIGHT:
An open-lipped beech wood vase and a brass horse, from the market in Denpasar, are distinctively displayed on stone pedestals.

LINKE SEITE:
Das elegante spiralförmige Firmenemblem von „Esprite Nomade" ist am Eingang eingelassen. Es symbolisiert den Gedanken, das Leben sei ein stetiger Prozess.

RECHTE SEITE:
Eine Schale aus Buchenholz und ein Messingpferd vom Markt in Denpasar, auf Steinsockeln stehend, verleihen dem Essbereich eine elegante Note.

PAGE DE GAUCHE:
L'élégant logo en volute de la marque «Esprite Nomade», qui est gravé dans la pierre à l'entrée, symbolise l'idée selon laquelle la «vie est un processus».

160

PAGE DE DROITE:
Sur des socles en pierre, une coupe en bois de hêtre et un cheval en laiton trouvés sur le marché de Denpasar donnent un cachet particulier au coin repas.

VILLA SAMADHANA

PABEAN

On the southeastern coast of Bali, north of Sanur, the Villa Samadhana can be found near remote beaches. There is no clear separation between the two homes that occupy a manicured jungle teaming with natural life. After crossing a bridge over deep ponds, teaming with koi, in order to enter the grounds, one finds roughly one hectare of rolling lawns with a banana plantation on the one side and a coconut grove on the other. The renowned landscape architect Trevor Hillier spontaneously designed this garden with ginger heliconias, tall grasses and five fish ponds. Using indigenous plants, he created an exotic garden setting for these modern, yet still warm, homes for two sisters and their families. The two villas, with wooden decks, rock gardens, objects of art and alternating opened and closed spaces, co-exist harmoniously. The view of the swimming pool extends dramatically to the ebbing ocean, and when dawn flutters over the coconut palms there is a sense of "harmony," the meaning of Samadhana.

A meditative stone Buddha is the first sight upon entering the Villa Samadhana – the word for harmony – through the door of the wooden gate.

Ein meditierender Steinbuddha begrüßt Besucher, wenn man durch die Holztür die Villa Samadhana betritt – der Name bedeutet „Harmonie".

Un bouddha de pierre dans une attitude méditative accueille le visiteur à l'entrée en bois de la villa Samadhana, la villa de l'harmonie.

Kaum ein Tourist verirrt sich an die Südostküste von Bali, wo man paradiesische Ruhe, versteckte Strände und die beiden Häuser der Villa Samadhana (was „Harmonie" bedeuted) findet. Die modernen und gemütlich eingerichteten Gebäude, in denen zwei Schwestern mit ihren Familien leben, stehen einträchtig Seite an Seite und machen ihrem Namen mit hübschen Holzterrassen, Steingärten, gesammelten Kunstgegenständen und offenen wie geschlossenen Räumen alle Ehre. Der Swimming-Pool mit seinen 25 Meter langen Bahnen leitet den Blick fast automatisch aufs blau glitzernde Meer, und der Garten trägt die Handschrift des Landschaftsarchitekten Trevor Hillier. Er gestaltete die Fläche spontan mit Ingwer, Helikonien und hohen Gräsern und verbindet das hektargroße Grundstück wie selbstverständlich mit einer Bananenplantage auf der einen und einem Kokoshain auf der anderen Seite. Vor der Villa Samadhana ist zudem ein tiefer Fischteich angelegt, über den sich eine Brücke spannt.

Sur le littoral sud-est de Bali, là où aucun touriste ne s'aventure, s'étendent les plages qui bordent les deux domiciles de la Villa Samadhana. Une fois passé le pont enjambant des bassins de carpes koï, on découvre les vastes pelouses de cette propriété d'un hectare flanquée d'une bananeraie d'un côté et d'une cocoteraie de l'autre. Trevor Hillier, architecte paysager de renom, a spontanément planté des gingembres, des balisiers, de hautes graminées et aménagé cinq bassins à poissons, créant un jardin exotique avec des espèces endémiques pour servir de cadre à ces deux maisons modernes mais accueillantes qui abritent les familles de deux sœurs. Elles coexistent en toute harmonie avec leurs ponts de bois, jardins de pierre, objets d'art de collection et leurs espaces tant ouverts que clos, bien que des styles très distincts se fassent jour sur ce site merveilleusement aménagé. La piscine de 25 mètres met en scène les flots de l'océan, face à la lumière fraîche de l'aube flottant sur les palmes des cocotiers qui dominent la résidence.

168

PREVIOUS DOUBLE PAGE:
The deck of the swimming pool with a curtained, four-poster, Madura bed seems to float above a huge crystalline swimming pool that almost seems to merge with the view of the ocean along the Ketewel coastline north of Sanur.

LEFT ABOVE:
A wooden door, with a mandala carved into it, is suspended above a collection of decorative figures from the Mentawai Islands in Sumatra.

LEFT BELOW:
An open bedroom corner overlooks the open garden, which was once village temple land.

RIGHT ABOVE:
A deck extending from one of the main houses overlooks ponds of tall grasses and water lilies.

RIGHT BELOW:
The thatched roof over one of the main open houses extends nearly to the pool.

VORIGE DOPPELSEITE:
Neben dem riesigen kristallklaren Swimming-Pool scheint das Himmelbett aus Madura zu schweben. Der Pool geht fließend über in den Blick auf das Meer an der Küste von Ketewel, nördlich von Sanur.

LINKS OBEN:
Eine hängende Holztür mit geschnitztem Mandala-Design bildet den Hintergrund einer Sammlung von Gegenständen von den Mentawai-Inseln Sumatras.

LINKS UNTEN:
Von einer offenen Schlafzimmerecke schaut man über den offenen Garten, der einstmals zum Tempelgelände des Dorfes gehörte.

RECHTE SEITE OBEN:
Eine Plattform vor einem der Hauptgebäude bietet einen Ausblick auf Teiche mit hohen Gräsern und Seerosen.

RECHTE SEITE UNTEN:
Das Grasdach eines der luftigen Hauptgebäude reicht bis in den Poolbereich hinein.

DOUBLE PAGE PRÉCÉDENTE:
Le pont sur lequel repose un lit de Madura à rideaux semble flotter sur l'immense piscine aux eaux limpides qui se fond dans la perspective de l'océan sur le littoral de Ketewel, au nord de Sanur.

EN HAUT, À GAUCHE:
Une porte suspendue en bois ornée d'un mandala sert de toile de fond à une collection d'accessoires très décoratifs provenant des îles Mentawai au large de Sumatra.

EN BAS, À GAUCHE:
Un coin chambre ouvert donne sur le jardin qui se trouvait autrefois dans l'enceinte du temple du village.

PAGE DE DROITE, EN HAUT:
Un pont dans le prolongement d'une des maisons principales donne sur les bassins dans lesquels poussent de hautes herbes et des nénuphars.

PAGE DE DROITE, EN BAS:
Le toit de chaume d'une maison principale ouverte et aérée recouvre partiellement le coin piscine.

VILLA SAMADHANA / PABEAN

A view of the extensive compound, with its variety of styles, from the swimming pool area where coconut trees reach maximum heights.

Ein Blick vom Swimming-Pool auf das ausgedehnte Gelände mit den beiden Villen und vereinzelten Kokospalmen, die ihre maximale Größe erreicht haben.

Vue depuis la piscine sur l´ensemble du site avec les deux villas s´élevant parmi les cocotiers qui ont atteint leur taille maximale.

170

LEFT ABOVE:
Malaysian-born and Singaporean-based landscape architect, Trevor Hillier, spontaneously designed the garden of banana plantations, lush shrubbery, tall grasses and walkways over ponds through jungle settings.

LEFT BELOW:
Wooden decks with open beams extend to views of horticultural wonder on a vast property of more than a hectare in size.

RIGHT PAGE ABOVE:
Inviting furnishings, including a Javanese bench hewn out of teak and Maduran sofas, are reflected in the terrazzo floors as well as in a Chinese celadon pot.

RIGHT PAGE BELOW:
Louvered doors embellish the clean lines and smooth textures in the light and airy bathroom.

LINKS OBEN:
Der Landschaftsarchitekt Trevor Hillier, geboren in Malaysia und ansässig in Singapur, entwarf ganz spontan diesen Garten mit Bananenplantagen, üppigem Gebüsch und hohen Gräsern inmitten einer Dschungellandschaft.

LINKS UNTEN:
Holzplattformen mit offenen Balkenkonstruktionen bieten Ausblicke auf ein Wunderland des Gartenbaus, das sich über ein mehr als ein Hektar großes Gelände erstreckt.

RECHTE SEITE OBEN:
Der Wohnbereich mit einer Teakholzliege aus Java und Sofas aus Madura wird aufgehellt durch den glänzenden Terrazzofußboden und ein antikes chinesisches Celadongefäß.

RECHTE SEITE UNTEN:
Helle Lamellentüren betonen die klaren Linien der glatten Oberflächen im luftigen Bad.

EN HAUT, À GAUCHE:
Trevor Hillier, architecte malaisien établi à Singapour, a conçu avec une grande spontanéité au milieu d'un décor de jungle avec ses bananiers, ses arbustes exubérants et ses hautes herbes ce jardin traversé par des chemins enjambant des bassins.

EN BAS, À GAUCHE:
Des ponts de bois ouverts se fondent dans ce paradis horticole sur une propriété de plus d'un hectare.

PAGE DE DROITE, EN HAUT:
Le salon avec un banc de Java taillé dans du teck et des sofas de Madura se reflète dans les sols de terrazzo et un céladon chinois ancien.

PAGE DE DROITE, EN BAS:
Des portes à claire-voie mettent en valeur les lignes pures des matériaux utilisés dans la salle de bains claire et spacieuse.

VILLA SAMADHANA / PABEAN

Verdant foliage and hanging heliconias frame the monolithic stone obelisks of the alfresco shower area in the garden bathroom, with river stones providing a natural ground surface.

Grünes Laubwerk mit hängenden Helikonien rahmt die monolithischen Obelisken der Freiluftdusche im Badezimmergarten ein, in dem Flusskies einen natürlichen Bodenbelag bildet.

Le feuillage vert relevé par le rouge des héliconias pendants sert de toile de fond aux montants monolithes de la douche en plein air dans le jardin-salle de bains où des galets constituent un revêtement de sol naturel.

174

VILLA SAMADHANA / PABEAN

176

LEFT ABOVE:
The bull's head Timor door carving and Tibetan tiger carpet are examples of some of the fine art objects displayed throughout the house.

LEFT BELOW:
Old wooden cart wheels become objects of art against the background of the textured walls.

RIGHT PAGE:
A carved wooden Naga sculpture is set between the full bookcases of the indoor library, which is frequented for research and study.

LINKS OBEN:
Der geschnitzte Stierkopf in der Tür aus Timor und der Tigerteppich aus Tibet sind Beispiele für einige der herrlichen Kunstgegenstände, die im gesamten Haus zur Schau gestellt werden.

LINKS UNTEN:
Alte hölzerne Wagenräder werden vor den strukturierten Wänden zu Kunstobjekten.

RECHTE SEITE:
Eine geschnitzte Naga-Skulptur aus Holz sitzt zwischen den beiden vollen Bücherregalen der Bibliothek, die der Forschung und dem Studium dient.

EN HAUT, À GAUCHE:
Deux objets d'art délicats parmi ceux exposés dans toute la maison: une sculpture en forme de tête de taureau provenant du Timor près de la porte et un tapis tibétain représentant un tigre.

EN BAS, À GAUCHE:
Ces roues de charrette en bois ressortant sur les ombres du mur finement texturé ont des qualités d'œuvres d'art.

PAGE DE DROITE:
Une sculpture sur bois naga s'est faufilée entre les étagères débordant de livres de la bibliothèque, où l'on se consacre à la recherche et à l'étude.

The billiard pavilion comes alive with waves of contemporary color on the wall behind the bar. The inspiration for the hand-painted wall came from a fabric designed by Paul Smith.

Moderne Farbwellen hinter dem Barbereich bringen Leben in den Billardpavillon. Die handbemalte balinesische Wand, wurde von einem Textildesign Paul Smiths inspiriert.

Derrière le bar du pavillon de billard, les vagues de couleurs d'un mur peint à la main inspiré d'un tissu du styliste Paul Smith donnent de la vie à la pièce.

VILLA BATUJIMBAR

SANUR

The exclusive beachfront compound of Batujimbar was inspired by Austrailian artist Donald Friend's palatial home in Sanur. Built in 1968, Friend moved into his residence on a date determined to be auspicious by a local astrologer. In 1979 the famous Ceylonese architect Geoffrey Bawa added his own touch to the premises, calling it "Pantai Sanur." Friend's extensive house staff, along with his remarkable miniature gamlan and art collections, contributed to his notoriety; his lifestyle was like that of a feudal lord. Visitors over the next twelve years included Desiderius Orban, Queen Soraya of Persia, Mick Jagger, the Duke of Edinburg, Gore Vidal and Prime Minister John Gorton. The traditional *kampung* buildings face a two-storied structure at the center. It has a museum on the lower level and an upper deck with views of the sea. The property was renovated by the architect and designer Ed Tuttle in 1985. Further renovations were undertaken during the late 1990s. Now water bubbles in fountains, while koi gracefully swim in ponds.

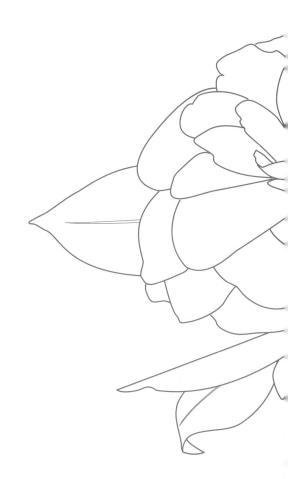

Koi flourish on Donald Friend's estate, where water has been a dominant theme since its construction in 1968.

Koi-Fische findet man hier zuhauf, denn seit den ersten Bauarbeiten im Jahre 1968 beherrschte das Thema Wasser diese Anlage des australischen Künstlers Donald Friend.

Les bassins regorgeant de carpes koi ont été un thème central de la propriété de l'artiste australien Donald Friend dès le début de sa construction, en 1968.

Die exklusive Villa Batujimbar steht direkt am Strand und ist ursprünglich ein Entwurf des australischen Künstlers Donald Friend aus dem Jahr 1968 (das Einzugsdatum ließ er damals übrigens von einem einheimischen Sterndeuter errechnen!). Gut ein Jahrzehnt später verlieh der ceylonesische Architekt Geoffrey Bawa dem Palast seine Handschrift und gab ihm den Namen „Pantai Sanur". Dank einer beachtlichen Domestiken-schar, eines eigenen Gamelan-Orchesters und einer bemer-kenswerten Kunstsammlung konnte Donald Friend hier wie ein Feudalherr residieren und eine illustre Gästeschar empfangen – darunter Kaiserin Soraya von Persien, den Herzog von Edin-burgh, Mick Jagger und Gore Vidal. Die traditionellen, als *kam-pung* bezeichneten Nebengebäude sind dem zweistöckigen Haupthaus zugewandt, das ein Museum beherbergt und aus dem Obergeschoss den Blick aufs offene Meer freigibt. 1985 und Ende der 1990er-Jahre wurde die Anlage vom Architekten und Designer Ed Tuttle rundum renoviert.

Cette propriété privée de Batujimbar, sur le front de mer, a pour point de départ la construction à Sanur en 1968, d'une mai-son aux allures de palais par l'artiste australien Donald Friend. En 1979, un célèbre architecte de Sri Lanka, Geoffrey Bawa, a ajouté sa touche au lieu et l'a baptisé «Pantai Sanur». L'armada de domestiques de Donald Friend, son «gamelan» miniature, orchestre indonésien, et sa remarquable collection d'œuvres d'art, ont contribué à lui forger une image de seigneur féodal bienveillant. Au cours des douze années qui ont suivi, il a reçu Desiderius Orban, la princesse Soraya, Mick Jagger, le duc d'Edimbourg, Gore Vidal, et le Premier ministre australien John Gorton. Des *kampung*, constructions traditionnelles, font face au bâtiment de deux étages agrémenté d'un musée en dessous et d'une terrasse en surplomb donnant sur la mer. Ce complexe étendu agrémenté de fontaines dans lesquelles évoluent des carpes koi a été rénové en 1985 par l'architecte et designer Ed Tuttle, puis une nouvelle fois à la fin des années 1990.

LEFT ABOVE:
Water-palace fountains in temple-inspired moats flank the museum building, designed by master Sri Lankan architect Geoffrey Bawa in 1975.

LEFT BELOW:
A modern wrought-iron chair upholstered in leather compliments the old Borneo mat beneath.

RIGHT ABOVE:
Architect Bawa's ingenious adaptation of the bale agung (assembly hall of the gods) became a museum on the first floor, housing an impressive collection of Friend's Balinese art works, and an open pavilion on top.

RIGHT BELOW:
A forceful Balinese deity guards and protects against evil spirits.

LINKS OBEN:
Nach dem Vorbild alter Tempel wird das Museumsgebäude von Palastspringbrunnen in Wassergräben umgeben. Die Entwürfe dazu schuf der ceylonesische Architekt Geoffrey Bawa 1975.

LINKS UNTEN:
Ein schmiedeeiserner, ledergepolsterter Armlehnstuhl ergänzt die alte Borneomatte darunter.

RECHTE SEITE OBEN:
Geoffrey Bawas einfallsreiche Adaption eines bale agung (Versammlungshalle der Götter) wurde zu einem Museum mit Friends eindrucksvoller Sammlung von balinesischen Kunstwerken. Darüber befindet sich ein offener Pavillon.

RECHTE SEITE UNTEN:
Eine mächtige balinesische Gottheit wacht und schützt vor bösen Geistern.

EN HAUT, À GAUCHE:
Des jets d'eau dans des fossés, inspirés de l'architecture religieuse, jouxtent le bâtiment du musée conçu en 1975 par l'architecte sri lankais Geoffrey Bawa.

EN BAS, À GAUCHE:
Mariage d'une chaise moderne en fer forgé tendue de cuir avec un tapis de Bornéo ancien.

EN HAUT, À DROITE:
L'adaptation ingénieuse par Bawa du bale agung, hall dans lequel s'assemblent les dieux, est devenue un musée au rez-de-chaussée et un pavillon ouvert à l'étage. Le musée abrite une impressionnante collection d'objets d'art balinais.

EN BAS, À DROITE:
Une divinité impressionnante de vigueur protège contre les esprits malins.

VILLA BATUJIMBAR / SANUR

A House on the Cliff

SOMA TEMPLE
PECATU

Vertiginous cliffs that challenge even the most athletic offer superb vantage points from which to see the diamond-studded reflections in the waves of the Java Sea. The barreling waves have made the surfing at the beaches along Bali's southern most coast, particularly in Bukit, world famous. Soma Temple, the American-born mother of an ardent surfing family, was one of the first expatriates to build a house here. It overlooks such spectacular surfing spots as Bingin, Dreamland, Impossible, Padang-Padang and, most famous of all, Ulu Watu. The latter also harbors one of Bali's most sacred temples. From Soma's open pavilion, perched on the edge of a cliff in the village of Pecatur, one can see the volcanoes of Java on a clear day, while to the north mighty Mt. Agung, the home of the Balinese gods, reigns mighty. Nestled among flowering trees in an otherwise dry area of the island, this charming Balinese style family home bustles with visitors and fellow surfers every weekend, while colorfully decorated fishing boats from Bali, and outer islands such as Sulawesi and Madura, dot the open sea.

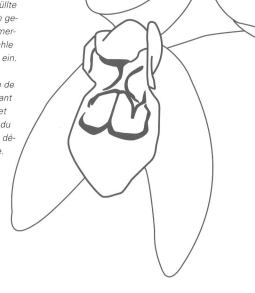

The bedroom bungalow, swathed with mosquito netting called kelambu and adorned with garden flowers, captures the sunset's half-light.

Der in kelambu genanntes Moskitonetzwerk gehüllte und mit Gartenblumen geschmückte Schlafzimmerbungalow fängt das fahle Licht der Dämmerung ein.

Cette chambre drapée de kelambu, voilages tenant lieu de moustiquaire, et agrémentée de fleurs du jardin capte la lumière déclinante du crépuscule.

Die Steilklippen von Bukit sind traumhafte Aussichtspunkte. Von hier aus bewundert man die glitzernden Wellen der Javasee, die sich aufrollen und kurz vor den kristallenen Stränden der Südküste Balis weiß schäumende Kämme bekommen – Surfer geraten schon beim bloßen Anblick ins Schwärmen. Die Amerikanerin Soma Temple, Matriarchin eines ganzen Clans begeisterter Wassersportler, war eine der ersten Ausländerinnen, die ein Haus nahe der spektakulären Spots von Bingin, Dreamland, Impossible, Padang-Padang und Ulu Watu baute. An klaren Tagen kann Soma von ihrem offenen Pavillon im Dorf Pecatu bis zu den Vulkanen der Nachbarinsel Java sehen; und den Norden beherrscht der mächtige Berg Agung, im Glauben der Einheimischen die Heimat der Götter. Das Wohnhaus selbst ist zwischen blühenden Bäumen eingebettet, bezaubert mit typisch balinesischem Stil und lebt im wahrsten Sinne des Wortes von den Bekannten und Surf-Freunden, die an jedem Wochenende zu Besuch kommen und das Leben genießen.

Du haut de falaises abruptes, un véritable défi même pour les athlètes, on embrasse du regard les reflets constellés de diamants des rouleaux transparents qui déferlent sur les plages d'une pureté cristalline des côtes les plus méridionales de Bali, dans une région connue sous le nom de Bukit. Soma Temple, cette Américaine mère de surfeurs passionnés, a compté parmi les premiers étrangers à se construire une maison dominant du haut d'une falaise des endroits bénis des surfeurs comme Bingin, Dreamland, Impossible, Padang-Padang et le célèbre Ulu Watu, qui abrite l'un des sanctuaires les plus sacrés de l'île. Quand le ciel est dégagé, on peut voir depuis le pavillon ouvert de Soma les volcans de Java et, au nord, l'impressionnant mont Agung, demeure des dieux de Bali. Nichée parmi les arbres fleuris, dans une partie normalement aride de l'île, cette charmante maison familiale de style balinais constituée de plusieurs constructions circulaires coiffées de chaume est envahie chaque week-end par des amis et des compagnons de surf.

LEFT:
The circular shaped master bedroom structure features rounded louvered shutters and a thatched Bali style roof.

RIGHT:
A window view of the garden including the lower pondok pavilion and ocean beyond.

LINKE SEITE:
Das kreisrunde Hauptschlafzimmer besitzt abgerundete Lamellenläden und ein mit Gras gedecktes Dach im balinesischen Stil.

RECHTE SEITE:
Ein Blick aus dem Fenster auf den Garten zeigt den unteren pondok-Pavillon und das Meer dahinter.

PAGE DE GAUCHE:
La construction circulaire abritant la chambre de maîtres se distingue par ses volets à claire-voie arrondis et son toit de chaume de style balinais.

PAGE DE DROITE:
Par la fenêtre donnant sur le jardin, on voit en contrebas le pondok, pavillon bas, et l'océan dans le lointain.

188

LEFT ABOVE:
Son Raven and his girl-friend Maddie gazing out at the Java Sea, waiting for the surf to come up on Bingin beach.

LEFT BELOW:
Daily offerings of assorted flowers are placed at the family shrine facing a northerly direction towards Mt. Agung.

RIGHT ABOVE:
The pondok pavilion is a focal spot built on the edge of the cliff overlooking the ocean and four spectacular surfing beaches below.

RIGHT BELOW:
The cat fancies a ceremonial drum from Central Java in the main house structure.

FOLLOWING DOUBLE PAGE LEFT:
A hand-painted tile from India depicting the Hindu god, Shiva, the Creator and Destroyer, is honored with "canang"offerings and fragrant incense.

FOLLOWING DOUBLE PAGE RIGHT ABOVE:
Sons and girlfriends surround Soma in a shot of the surfing family.

FOLLOWING DOUBLE PAGE RIGHT BELOW:
The main house, facing the ocean, is illuminated at dusk's golden hour.

LINKS OBEN:
Sohn Raven und seine Freundin Maddie blicken hinaus auf die Javasee und warten darauf, dass die Flut die passenden Wellen zum Surfen vor dem Strand von Bingin bringt.

LINKS UNTEN:
Täglich werden diverse Blumen im Familien-schrein als Opfer darge-bracht. Das Gebäude ist nach Norden, zum Berg Agung hin, ausgerichtet.

RECHTE SEITE OBEN:
Der pondok-Pavillon und allgemeine Treffpunkt wurde am Rande der Klippe gebaut, wo man einen Blick auf gleich vier spektakuläre Surf-Strände genießt.

RECHTE SEITE UNTEN:
Die Katze findet Gefallen an einer Zeremonientrom-mel aus Zentraljava im Hauptgebäude.

FOLGENDE DOPPELSEITE LINKS:
Eine handbemalte Kachel aus Indien stellt den Hindugott Shiva dar. Der Schöpfer und Zerstörer wird mit canang-Opfern und duftendem Weihrauch geehrt.

FOLGENDE DOPPELSEITE RECHTS OBEN:
Auf diesem Familienfoto des Surferklans ist Soma von ihren Söhnen und deren jeweiligen Freundin-nen umgeben.

FOLGENDE DOPPELSEITE RECHTS UNTEN:
Das Haupthaus ist zum Meer hin ausgerichtet und wird zur goldenen Stunde der Abenddämmerung hell erleuchtet.

EN HAUT, À GAUCHE:
Raven, le fils de la maison, et sa petite amie Maddie observent la mer de Java, attendant la marée qui leur apportera les vagues propices au surf sur la plage de Bingin.

EN BAS, À GAUCHE:
Les offrandes quoti-diennes de fleurs sont disposées près de l'autel familial orienté au nord, en direction du mont Agung.

PAGE DE DROITE, EN HAUT:
Véritable point de mire, le pondok s'élève au bord de la falaise surplombant quatre plages de surf spectaculaires.

PAGE DE DROITE, EN BAS:
Dans le bâtiment principal, le chat apprécie tout par-ticulièrement un tambour de cérémonie provenant du centre de Java.

PAGE SUIVANTE À GAUCHE:
Cette céramique indienne peinte à la main représen-tant le dieu hindou Shiva, créateur et destructeur, est vénérée par des offrandes de canang et d'encens parfumé.

PAGE SUIVANTE À DROITE, EN HAUT:
Les fils de la maison et leurs petites amies entou-rent Soma sur cette photo de famille des surfers.

PAGE SUIVANTE À DROITE, EN BAS:
La maison principale face à l'océan s'illumine à la nuit tombante.

Addresses / Adressen / Adresses

ARCHITECTS

ARCHITECT: CHEONG YEW KUAN
BA, BArch, MSIA
45 Cantonment Road
Singapore, 089748
PHONE: +65 673 55995
FAX: +65 673 88295

STUDIO: CANGGAHWANG
Banjar Begawan
Payangan – Bali
PHONE: +62 361 978777
FAX: +62 361 978787
E-MAIL: area@indo.net.id

ARCHITECT: ED TUTTLE
Design Realization
71, rue des Saints Pères
75006 Paris, France
PHONE: +33 142 226577
EMAIL: dretcm@compuserve.com

LANDSCAPE ARCHITECT: TREVOR HILLIER
BSc. MPhil. ALI SILA
One Degree North Landscape Architects
68 Jalan Bahasa
Singapore 299295
MOBILE: +65 961 50873
EMAIL: onedegreenorth@pacific.net.sg

BALI STUDIO:
Jalan Bumi Ayu 11A
Sanur, 80228, Denpasar
PHONE: +62 361 282286
FAX: +62 361 283948
MOBILE: +62 812 3918009

DESIGNERS

JOHN HARDY JEWELRY DESIGN
Banjar Baturning, Desa Mambal, Badung
PHONE: +62 361 469888

FAX: +62 361 469898/469899
EMAIL: john@johnhardy.com
www.johnhardy.com

LINDA GARLAND DESIGN
The International Bamboo Foundation
Environmental Bamboo Foundation of Indonesia
Jl. Nyuh Gading, Banjar Nyuh Kuning, Ubud – Bali
PHONE: +62 361 974028
FAX: +62 361 974029
EMAIL: info@lindagarland.com
www.lindagarland.com

AMIR RABIK DESIGNS
Komp. Istana Kuta Galeria
Blok Vallet 2 No. 11
Jl. Patih Jelantik, Kuta – Bali
PHONE: +62 361 769286
FAX: +62 361 769186
EMAIL:rabik@indo.net.id

FURNITURE

WARISAN
Jl. Raya Padang Luwih 198
Banjar Tegal Jaya, Dalung, Kuta – Bali
PHONE: +62 361 421752
FAX: +62 361 421214
EMAIL: sales@warisan.com
www.warisan.com

KEMARIN HARI INI
Jl. Raya Basangkasa No. 1200BC
PHONE: +62 361 730508
FAX: +62 361 730508
EMAIL: gundul@eksadata.com

JONATHAN FURNITURE
Jl. Raya Kerobokan No. 86
Br. Taman Kuta – Bali
PHONE: +62 361 739563
FAX: +62 361 751584

EMAIL: java_antique@hotmail.com
www.jonathan-furniture.com

TARITA FURNITURE
Jl. Padang Luwih No. 100X
Kerobokan, Kuta – Bali
PHONE: +62 361 411773
FAX: +62 361 426344
EMAIL: info@tarita.com
www.tarita.com

WAKALOUKA INDUSTRIES
Jean Jacques Audureau
Wood Design and Production
Jl. Padang Kartika 5X – Bali
Padang Sambian Klod, Denpasar
PHONE: +62 361 262388
FAX: +62 361 429995
E MAIL: wakaloka@indosat.net.id

INTERIOR & SOFT FURNITURE

HAVELI
Jl. Basangkasa 15
Seminyak – Bali
PHONE: +62 361 737160
FAX: +62 361 724497
EMAIL: haveli@equinoxtrading.com
www.equinoxtrading.com/haveli

JENGGALA KERAMIK
Jl. Uluwatu II
Jimbaran – Bali
PHONE: +62 361 703311
FAX: +62 361 703312
EMAIL: info@jenggala-bali.com
www.jenggala-bali.com

HANANTO LLOYD
Jl. Raya Sayan, Ubud – Bali
PHONE: +62 361 7429337
FAX: +62 361 971916

EMAIL: info@hanantolloyd.com
www.hanantolloyd.com

THE ORCHARD
Jl. Oberoi 33 X
Legian – Bali
PHONE: +62 361 736724
FAX: +62 361 736725
EMAIL: info@ibaldesigns.com
www.ibaldesigns.com

THE MEGUMI GALLERY
Jl. Pratama No. 61 Nusa Dua
PHONE: +62 361 775620
FAX: +62 361 774902
EMAIL: megumi-bali@dps.centrin.net.id

DELIGHTING
Jl. Gatot Subroto Barat 99
Kerobokan, Kuta – Bali
PHONE: +62 361 412194
FAX: +62 361 420512
EMAIL: info@de-lighting.com
www.de-lighting.com

ON THE OTHER SIDE
Jl. Lasmana (Oberoi)
Seminyak – Bali
PHONE/FAX: +62 361 731342
EMAIL: grdmas@dps.centrin.net.id
www.baliontheotherside.com

GALERI ESOK LUSA
Jl. Raya Basangkasa
Seminyak – Bali
PHONE/FAX: +62 361 735262
EMAIL: gundul@eksadata.com

LEOLLE
SHOW ROOM:
Jl. Raya Kerobokan No. 11, Br. Taman
Kerobokan – Bali
PHONE: + 62 361 732234
FAX: +62 361 730259

RETAIL SHOP:
Jl. Monkey Forest
Ubud – Bali
PHONE: + 62 361 971547
EMAIL: info@leollebali.com
www.leollebali.com

MORRESBALI INTERIOR ACCESSORIES PURCHASER
Anna Audureau
Jl. By Pass Ngurah Rai 100 A
Suwung Kauh, Denpasar Seletan – Bali
PHONE/ FAX: +62 361 725303
EMAIL: morres@indosat.net.id

ANTIQUES

KARMA GALLERY
PO Box 3403
Denpasar – Bali

KUSIA GALLERY
Jl. Raya Sanggingan No. 99X
Ubud – Bali
PHONE/FAX: +62 361 973113
EMAIL: kusia99@hotmail.com

KONDERATU GALLERY
Jl. Uluwatu II No. 101X
Jimbaran – Bali
PHONE: +62 361 702995
FAX: +62 361 702994
EMAIL: intracip@indo.net.id

TEXTILES

DUTA SILK
Jl. Dewi Sartika Blok I no 1. (Next to Matahari),
Denpasar - Bali
PHONE/FAX: +62 361 232818

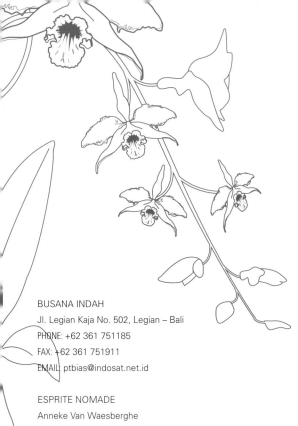

BUSANA INDAH
Jl. Legian Kaja No. 502, Legian – Bali
PHONE: +62 361 751185
FAX: +62 361 751911
EMAIL: ptbias@indosat.net.id

ESPRITE NOMADE
Anneke Van Waesberghe
Jl. Rsi Markandya II No. 17 Payogan
Ubud – Bali
PHONE: +62 361 976630/1
FAX: +62 361 976630
EMAIL: info@espritenomade.com
www.espritenomade.com

BOUTIQUES

BIASA
Jl. Raya Seminyak No. 34-3
Kuta – Bali
PHONE: +62 361 730945
FAX: +62 361 730766
EMAIL: biasa@biasabali.com
www.biasabali.com

PAUL ROPP
OFFICE ADDRESS:
Jl. Pengubengan No. IX
Depan LP. Kerobokan Kuta – Bali
PHONE: +62 361 730023
FAX: +62 361 730022
EMAIL: info@paulropp.com
www.paulropp.com

MILO'S
Kuta Square
Kuta – Bali
PHONE: +62 361 754081
FAX: +62 361 753996
EMAIL: miloshop@idola.net.id

HOTELS

UMA UBUD
Jl. Raya Sanggingan, Banjar Lungsiakan,
Kedewatan – Ubud – Bali
PHONE: +62 361 972448
FAX: +62 361 972449
EMAIL: res.ubud@uma.como.bz
www.uma.como.bz

BEGAWAN GIRI ESTATE
Banjar Begawan, Desa Melinggih Kelod,
Payangan – Ubud – Bali
PHONE: +62 361 978888
FAX: +62 361 978889
EMAIL: reservations@begawan.com
www.begawan.com

TAMAN SELINI
Desa Pemuteran – Singaraja
PHONE: +62 362 94746
FAX: +62 362 93449
EMAIL: selinibalipmt@yahoo.com
www.selinibali.com

RENTAL VILLAS

BALI TROPICAL VILLAS
Anita Lococo
Gang Lalu No. 7
Seminyak – Bali
PHONE/FAX: +62 361 732083
EMAIL: anita@bali-tropical-villas.com
www.bali-tropical-villas.com

IMPRINT

PAGE 2:
*View of the bar in Villa
Samadhana, Pabean*

SEITE 2:
*Blick auf den Barbereich
der Villa Samadhana,
Pabean*

PAGE 2:
*Vue sur le bar de la Villa
Samadhana, Pabean*

FRONT COVER:
*Living area in Cynthia and
John Hardy's house, Ubud*

UMSCHLAGVORDERSEITE:
*Sitzgruppe im Haus von
Cynthia und John Hardy,
Ubud*

COUVERTURE:
*Groupe de fauteuils dans
la maison de Cynthia et
John Hardy, Ubud*

BACK COVER:
*Alfresco shower area at
Linda Garland's Panchoran
Estate, Ubud*

UMSCHLAGRÜCKSEITE:
*Freiluftdusche bei Linda
Garland, Panchoran
Estate, Ubud*

DOS DE COUVERTURE:
*La douche en plein air
chez Linda Garland,
Panchoran Estate, Ubud*

© 2005 TASCHEN GmbH
Hohenzollernring 53, D–50672 Köln
www.taschen.com

To stay informed about upcoming TASCHEN titles,
please request our magazine at www.taschen.com/
magazine or write to TASCHEN, Hohenzollernring 53,
D–50672 Cologne, Germany, Fax +49-221-254919,
contact@taschen.com. We will be happy to send you a
copy of our magazine which is filled with information
about all of our books.

Concept, edited and layout by
Angelika Taschen, Cologne
Designed and illustrated by
dieSachbearbeiter, Berlin
General Project Management by
Stephanie Bischoff, Cologne
French translation by Christèle Jany, Cologne
German translation by Dr. Thomas Kinne, Nauheim

Printed in Italy

ISBN 978–3–8228–4600-1
(Edition with English / German cover)
ISBN 978–3–8228–4602-5
(Edition with French cover)

**TASCHEN'S
HOTEL BOOK SERIES**
Edited by Angelika Taschen

"'Decorator porn', a friend calls it, those sensuous photograph books of beautiful houses. Long on details and atmosphere and packed with ideas, this is a bountiful look at beautiful but unpretentious homes in the place where 'everything is founded on the link between beauty and well-being'. It's easy to linger there."
The Virginian-Pilot, USA

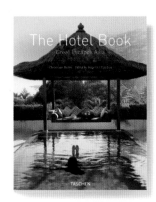
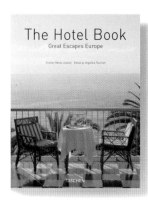

IN PREPARATION:
The Hotel Book –
Great Escapes Central America

The Hotel Book –
Great Escapes Cities

The Hotel Book –
Great Escapes Germany

The Hotel Book –
Great Escapes Italy

The Hotel Book –
Great Escapes Spain

The Hotel Book –
Low Budget

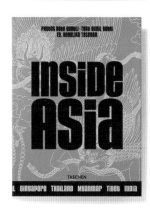
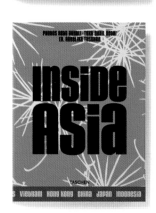
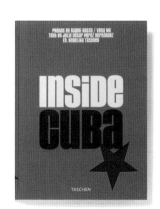

**TASCHEN'S
LIVING IN SERIES**
Edited by Angelika Taschen

IN PREPARATION:
Living in China

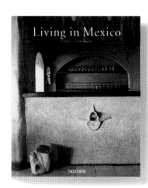
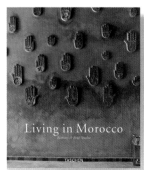